# Poem Attics

## Quantum Poetry

Jason Brenton Gore

ISBN: 9798862257786

THIS IS DEDICATED TO MY MOM…
**LINDA LARSON**

Who said, "Writers starve in the streets every day!"
Well? Don't be silly, mom.
Writers can starve anywhere they'd like.
It's a free country!

"You can't depend on your eyes.
When your imagination is out of focus.."

—Mark Twain

# CONTENTS

# PREFACE

## The 2-in-1 Style Of Poetry

Firstly, I must remark on the multiple ways in which one can read these poems. Although I've renamed this style of poetry several times, for clarity's sake, I think the "2-in-1" style explains this method in the simplest form. I've linguistically, romantically, semantically, repetitively, and literally hacked the English language to create this "2-in-1" poetry by manipulating the weaknesses and inconsistencies of the language to my advantage. It's ambiguity within structure via syntactic choice!! For example, I've used words containing multiple and differing definitions or homonyms, as well as words that function as different parts of speech, regardless of meaning.

To make this poetic method as simple as possible to understand: Read the poem once across as usual. Then reread *one* side of the poem as a column, down to its bottommost line, and continue to read from the top of the *other* side until the end of the poem at its furtherest down, right position. Here's a quick example poem to illustrate this idea:

**POEM TITLE**

**Read** **Down**
**Each** **Then**
**Row…** **Across!**

1.) The first word order can be read across line by line, as normal:
"**Read Down Each Then Row… Across!**"

2.) Yet, the alternative word order, split into separate rows, reads:
"**Read Each Row… Down Then Across!**"

This is not an easy task to accomplish while maintaining a reasonably coherent, grammatically accurate idea. Fortunately, poetic license affords the opportunity to suspend some of these literary laws for the sake of art, but be aware that I've put a lot of time into the construction of these poems and their structures (many years and decades for some of these works). If I've seemed to misuse or misspell any words of text, it was by choice and for a thematic purpose or a stylistically designated reason.

Although directionally diverse, by changing the order of the words, this method can also change the meaning of the poem in a less paradoxical manner than expected. Sometimes, the alternate path in the order of a poem's words acts as a reinforcement to the initial theme's supposed interpretation surmised from the first path's reading order.

Of course, there are many poems in this text that have more than two halves of dissected lines to follow, just as there are many that follow the traditionally normal, single approach for reading and comprehending verse. Some have objective and apparent ways to read them, while others follow more blended and tricky directions to follow. My vision through this work is to evolve poetry into a digitally enhanced form and bring a style that fits a more modern, twenty-first century approach to the artform. Following this idea, I have a companion **YouTube Channel** for this book:

**https://youtube.com/@Poemattics**

The channel isn't fully complete, and as of 2023, the production isn't exactly as professional as it will be. I plan on having more complex versions of the physical copies of this book in the future as well, but for art's sake, these poems should be published and able to stand on their own merits! On the other hand, the YouTube Channel still contains a growing number of narrated and scored videos of fun poems from this book with which you can follow the appearance of each poem's different pathways with the narration as you compare the process to the physical versions of the ones in this book!

In essence, the obvious purpose of this introduction is to explain the method of reading and processing the poetry found on these pages and to provide insight into the unique style of the "2-in-1" poetry presented in this collection. As the poet, I aim to push the boundaries of traditional poetry through the use of linguistic manipulation, semantic ambiguity, as well as grammatical and numerical devices to offer the reader multiple nuanced, interpretations and paths to follow, allowing for a more interactive and dynamic reading experience.

Ultimately, my hope is that the reader will appreciate the intricate craftsmanship and depth of meaning in each poem, and perhaps even be inspired to explore their own creativity in new and unconventional ways. I thank you for joining me and taking the time to let my art entertain you!

# The Singularity of Art
## (Quantum Poetry and Poetic Superposition)

The "Singularity of Art" is an idea that encompasses all forms of art (painting, music, animation, literature, cinema, etc.), to be perceived by all five faculties of physical senses (taste, touch, sight, sound, and smell). This concept involves producing a piece of analog or digital artwork, or some combination of the two, that transcends any one medium (physically or digitally) by inherently using all different forms of media simultaneously. In physics, "quantum" refers to the minimum unit of any physical entity involved in an interaction. Quantum computing differs from "classical" computing by manipulating the typical binary digit system of either an "0" or "1" (yes/no, true/false, etc.) from the classical bit into the quantum bit or qubit. The bytes of a classical computer consist of these bits arranged in a series (for example, "0" or "1" in the first bit, then "0" or "1" in the next bit, and so on). A qubit uses superposition to manipulate the bit to be both "0" and "1" simultaneously through vertical and horizontal polarization of subatomic particles like electrons or photons (the particles of light). Hence, the process of qubits operates in a series *and* in parallel simultaneously.

Compared to a classical computer processor that uses a series of bits to computationally run or "read" information through a single, straightforward sequence of events, these actions resemble the typical, linear manner in which a human reads a poem or passage of prose.

By a fortunate accident, the concept of quantum processing and superposition aligns almost perfectly with how the dual nature of poetry can be "processed" (or run) or, more accurately, read. Following this idea, quantum poetry or poetic superposition allows for multiple poems to exist within the same text, using a similar context as a quantum mechanism might. Once an audio/video book is completed to accompany this printed book, complete with music and soundscapes, and featuring the vertical and horizontal polarization through multiple narrations of each poem, the idea of a poetic singularity will hopefully come to fruition and become more easily recognizable!

# PROEM

## 1, 2, & 4:
**The Magic 3 and what you don't see!**

*From a passing look at my poetry, the obvious and purposefully emblematic shape of each poem, initially rises to view. Peering just underneath that clear, blue-watered look over the poetry from the surface level of words bubbling up together to create abstract and discernible concrete structures, the odd misuse of punctuation and spelling, as well as individual letters and numerals (especially 1, 2, and 4), will most likely be the next distinction repetitively emerging from the shallow end of the text and initially catching the reader's eyes. The substitution of these number characters instead of the use of their homophonically related grammatical counterparts or their homonymic "siblings" (or the literal 'words' the numbers might represent) is not the result of laziness, not a shallow attempt at attaining some form of unique style, not a confusing aim at ambiguity, nor another cheap way to manipulate the text of the poem to shape the image in which the characters and words of the text are intended to form. Rather, this inconsistent use of numerals and characters instead of using the conventional, homophonically corresponding word is precisely a combination of all previously and seemingly discounted examples.*

*Unfortunately for the reader, if this substitution process is disconcerting, I also tend to do this with some irony yet randomly with serious sobriety, albeit unambiguously. It's up to the reader to decide which way to perceive these vague issues when they arise. In the defense of my poetry and my unusual aesthetic style, I do not think lightly of these artistic decisions. I've spent nearly thirty years working on this poetry, wrestling with each and every word, character, or numeric choice, use or unused punctuation, font size, spacing, etc. Also, I follow, study, and believe in numerology, angel numbers, and synchronology as part of my spiritual makeup; so to say that these numerical devices placed into my work have nothing to do with my poetry, would be an outright lie and a self-sacrilege.*

*Furthermore I think of these poems as my babies. I love them! I have taken so much time and care with each one of them that it almost saddens and frightens me to publish them. Conversely, that would be a cowardly waste… as all art is intended to be a trasnformative joy, communicating its own emotional language across all barriers! On a deeply personal level, while still protected from the outside world and the prying eyes of criticism and interpretation, where they must stand on their own, only being what I have made them to be, I fear they won't seem alive to me anymore. Not as they do in my private care; where they're continually growing and changing… living… as I see fit…*

*None of this essay is an excuse for any form of shortcomings within my art. I just thought that if one decided to read this essay, then they would have been compelled to have done so, by the act of taking interest in my poetry, whether academically or purely from an angle of entertainment. It's not necessarily uncommon for a writer or artist to explain the parameters or partial thesis of their work. Edgar Allen Poe wrote an essay defining the structure (and basically the rules) of the Short Story, in which he invented. Not only did Salvador Dali almost thematically unveil each of his paintings via their poignant and lengthy descriptive titles, but additionally he wrote elaborate descriptions to accompany each piece as well as writing extensively about the themes, the emotions, the imagery, and the personal origins to a multiple number of his paintings. Other artist have held seminars or gave extensive interviews in which they were seemingly, very transparent with all conceivable aspects of their works. William Faulkner held so many seminars at the University of Mississippi (or better known as Ole' Miss in Oxford, Mississippi, having also been his home), that he could have been teaching his own class and handing course hours out to the students in attendance as credits toward their degrees!*

*As for comparisons with other books of poetry or prose, many writers have written introductions or prefaces that explain their creative process or themes that their work explores. For example, T.S. Eliot's "The Waste Land" includes a preface in which he explains the historical and cultural context of the poem, as well as his own creative process. Additionally, Allen Ginsberg's "Howl" includes a preface in which he explains the inspiration behind the poem and its themes.*

*In summation, if this introduction to my poetry seems too winded or expansive, it was only clarity for the reader's sake and not convoluted rhetoric originating from a place of insecurity. This, I promise with metaphoric fingers crossed (not because I'm outright and sarcastically deceiving you with this prosaic fodder, but pertaining to the duality, and sometimes conflicting nature of the poetry, itself, I find it a somewhat necessary formality in hopes that this disclaimer will provide some understanding for the reader and clear any air around such an unusual stylistic approach to the poetic art form!)*

Jason B. Gore
Friday, October 13, 2023

# Good and Bad

in

a slip—
of your
breath—

kNot
head—
ing

out

# Before I Was Left & After I Was Right

before
me,
nothing
so much
but
*love* . . .

You
and
I
did it
only
without
understanding . . . it

left
the
wanted
need
to leave
. . . *love*

# Heaven and Hell

"In me thou see'st the glowing of such fire
That on the ashes of his youth doth lie."
— William Shakespeare
Sonnet 73

Remind me of Heaven—
A dark piece of mind,
Exterminated,
To the colors of
A revealing
Yet dissected
Exoskeletal thought,
Places the
Best...

And, of course, Hell
where the heart is
gently turning
inflamed roses to
truth spoken,
portions of
buried
pieces that
...puzzle

Sunlight, shattered by tapered, disconnected clouds and eyelash views,
Into a center, a pupil wrinkled by a smile.
The devil's love is eating toward a cigarette butt.

Skins...
With the time
Abstracted
And
Memory
Lost
Forever
To the fusil,
Hard-fisted contingency
To find the forgiving...

...Age
wrapped around
trees,
broken
from
days
gone
and driven into a
(known)
grave.

# Love and Hate

When **you** were Like a cool sun that **bent**
With my thoughts to the **shape** of my head
Like a pillow **to** my falling mind, I slipped **in**to love w/
Your heart dripping **blood** all over. . . **you**.

**My Hands**

**Dirty** from cleaning and torn from scratching broken surfaces
Were listening with clever and disillusive blindness to your fainting
Pulse. Your horn and engine, shifting, quieted, passing intonothing.
I'm sosorry I **Can*Ever*** See you
Look this way. Not understanding a great deal, like Thinking
*What* You know
About *me*? These blistered remains. This brain withered like
Nothing ever could be dark and **black**
like your. . . roses

**Touch**

Me with the **lost**
Years and with shaky ***stir*** these emotions in a bowl, and Spring
Your cold spoon screaming across the hot, metal bottom of my heart,
Loving your fist and beating holes in the **night** clouds
The smile on the breaking stars of

**Your Face**

Tortured to the point of tears
racing away from your imperfect eyes, and it is
from me, you find a good and **bad** feeling,
The **way** to forget how
it should be. . . to remember

**Again...!**

# *Pretty***Ugly**

This has presumed
Beauty: to be
Taster of perfumed
Fruity candy
Smells of entombed
Booty, in the
Chaser of the cocooned
Nutty- -slutty
Fuddy-Duddy- -Study-Buddy
Floozy
This has assumed
It's story to be
Left Right?
To the Consumed
Romantic in the
Moon, the bite!
Overlooked The wound
Will be freely
Dubious and.... Outta-sight
In Love!

**^**

**|**

# -RaiNBow-

Point of Hue ^ Is NOT Right
Next To You ^ To Shoot Rain
Bended Light ^ Skyward Like
Upside Down ^ Arrow Tears
Turns Height ^ Colored Nite
To Blow Out ^ Line Of Sight
—InTo The Vertigo Of Existence A R**A**CE W/Our Eyes Only To *Separate*—
Umbrellas **\W/** Spectrums
& A Look **A** Like This
**WAY**
**TO LOVE**

# iNsIdEoUt

NO

this torn tuxedo
evolving sorrow
backs words
to hearsay,
thought, that
was her throwing eyes
buying goods

turns innuendo
into tomorrow
backwards
heresy was
that thought
blowing careless assault
by good byes

IF

I miss taking
Lives
to be loved
so still
my lover
kisses
on my forehead
with loose touch

mistaken
lives
love to be
stealing
I love her
kisses
for my head
will lose touch

AND

you win
quit quitting
my mind sees
as that

when you
end beginning
my mind's sea
that has

OR

a way
to never
land
rightsideout

away
never
landing
insidewrong

over BUT out

# Broke iN

I see how you're burgling me!
Sneaky robber peaking in my heart.
You're thought...........holding me hostage.
Locked inside.....................I'll have your key!
My messy nights.....................holes in the dark sky
Your wit & all that shit.........I love it; but understand
This is mine!................................................What is ours?
The question.......is This................This is........All of our love;
Belonging to...........both.................of us!........Knocks@doors
Shapes we take.........in................to...........one or the other's
Lives for pleasure.............................homes in the mind
You can jiggle my....................handle, shake w/ care.
Bewildered soul.......................I'm F'n lost 'n you!!
You let me in............I'm...........not getting out
Escape was..........w/out..........an option
Its own..........way-out..........to tell
Prison..........stories to.........me
Built for..........freedom's...........shit!
Heroes.............glorious grins...............If
Owning words meant to open up our hearts
I'll make a break for it and break the hinges off
The line crossed and the seal broke in and our house
Is our guarded romance constructed out of trust and cut
From a portal peering at paradise that only love dreams about
Looking far from an outside glimpse into the greatest feelings ever
Caught in the breeze of the universe so let me in sweetly so I can be alive
Near the fiery lookouts for our lives & we can enjoy the outlooks of your love.

# **Slow.... ...speeD**

You can't spell "emotion" w/out motion, retarded,
with silly thoughts. I know I'm kicking my own heart
too much. It tricks love's way awake, and I, foolishly, wait
around counting
WIRE——————————————LESS
figures on times
when I look, they say, "I guess that's the brakes?" and I'm mumbling it
with lifeless expressions. "How do I stop?" I want her eyes lifted open
slowly like a garage door, to free her heart from the cage of bones that
keeps her from bouncing through my sky... I'm a wreck and she's stuck
in traffic b/c I'm playing chicken w/a turtle's head... Can she love this?
This shell of a man; who has distanced himself like a dim reflection in a
mirror across a deserted room. I do believe her oasis is a genuine thirst
for a man like me to soak my eyes in more than a mirage's quick sands.
I trust myself less than I see her but her child-like grin pushes me in, to
things that were once not in my way, as if I were a dysfunctional robot,
and she were my maker. I feel crushed w/elevated *wait* Understanding
that I have never taken her lips to mine her affections never closed her
mouth w/tear-wet palms nor heard her shaky voice raspy w/ sleep. My
Headlights are off now, the slow road is gone & my head is light. Speed
W/out friction curving Warps the lives that
Can't trust love to last Long with her Heart
An Inability to stop its ——ENERGY—— Traveling too fast in
Inertia...solely passing Time...I left it w/out
Myself losing purpose Knowing I missed it.
I'm only an old blind hitcher froze like an aging mime on some desolate
Dirigible dirtroad: Thumbs up w/out a soul to sell to catch a ride to hell.

# Heart To Heart

You.... ....Baby
Tickle On My Soul!
My Love For You Color
Sounds All Mermaid Up For You,
Like You Pick-pocket A Heart's
Treating All My Love Like Love
Lives Forever & I Will
W/Love For Us Carry On
You Scare Me Smiling, You're
Silly Smart
Girl Help
Yourself To me.
Your Eyes Burning
Changing Me Good
To Warm A Romantic
Thought Feeling
Your Lips Sticking
Out Surround My Heart
Together Always
With You
And
Me

# BYE POLAR EYES

It was such A
Poor Pour
The Alcohol Burned like Gas And The Ice Melted The Glass
Frozen Raining
From A Some
What (I) Digested (I) Hate
Looked Mucilaginous Ahead
Of Fate OtherWise For Us
Untasted Saline Goggled View Points Two Ways
Too Symbolic
For Symmetrical
Designs for 2 Lines
It was such A
Nurturing So——So Unnatural
That We Turned A Wet Smile In
As Slicker Tears Evaporated
Like Ghost Before Dying

# THESEYES

There is A Place Near Her Face
Hidden Behind
Her Cheek,
A Place Where
Her Chin Her Ear
And Her
Neck Meet
It's A Beautiful Bermuda Triangle
Of Secret Dreams Where
She Speaks Her Mind
Listens to Her
Heart
And Breathes Life Into Me!

# ...MirrOrriM...

Renew A Sight! Reteach A New LeveL When A Cheater Ties A Winner!

Funny
Hell...
Cuts
Any
Peels
A-part
Livid
Smoke
A Lit
Sore
Skin
I'm
God
Nose
Late
On
Zion
I'd
Dare
Lips
Slip
Cool
Kiss
Face
Soap
I'd Lie

Enough
...Lay
Stuck
In A
Sleep
Trap-A
Devil
Comes
Till A
Rose
Nics
My
Dog
Sewn
Tale
No-
No I's
Dye
Read
Spill
Pills
Look
Sick
Safe
Pose
I'll Die

When I Mite Retire! Am I Mad? Wow! Damn, I'm A Writer! Time I Knew!

# Mental Patience

I've been to visit Horror Houses & Bent the Mirrors
Cut-Off All From Scissors
Kicked **And** **Eye** Scream
Outta **Laugh** **Alotta** "Love"
Things **For** **You** Crazy
sUnreal Heartsy
Timing **A** Mused
If **Meaning** **Endings** In
Iamb See**ming to be Dream**ing From
Dumber **Loose Smiles** Leaving
Me Clowny Town Alone
With A Fake-Frown-Make-Shift-Style Of Our Own!

# ~~A M A Z E M I N T I N W O R D S~~

Always All—Ways Follow Your Heart-—-OPEN-—-Lead By Ex Ample Act Shuns Speech
Volume-wise of Love Loss
Lesser Than The Grader Of Rulers Degrees In Life And Time Man
Aged Longer Than We Thought We Knew Were Newer
Where It had Worn Us Down To
The Ground Back Up To Norm All
Procedures Wear By Or We
Taught & It Had To Be Behaving Like Most Of Us
Wants To Be Come For Table Too Close To Close Two
Now It's Our First And Last Chance Early Birds Flew Coach To The
Game Face Off Mooning Eyes After A Weight
Lift Of Spirit On The Other Hand Too Heavy Handed To Wave
By TO My
Hi Fly By Hi Fi On My Wi Fi By Hi Time I Find My Nite Lite And Eye
X2 Multiplied Inside My Rite Mind Set Of Fine Dining Ware Like
Tries Sky Diving In If I Apply Myself And Try Not To Cry Wolves
Hiding In The Hide of A Sheep In Plain Site Of A Posing A
Problem A Definition
Of Our Certainty To Choose 1 In A Specifically Inclined Life
Style Over Reasonable Timed Decisions To Understand
Planned
—Escape A Responsibility Of Entering-—-EXIT-—-This Path Of Logical Sin And Sorrow—

# A BUTTERFLY'S LULLABY

WE'D BEEN
BUZZED BYABEE
BEFORE HANDING OVER THE DAYBREAK BACK TO
TIGHTENED GRIPS OF NIGHTFALLING OVER
REINCARNATION WAS ONLY THE REALLOCATION OF SUN
BUMBLING & BEGGING ABOUT OUR FLOWERS
BUT THERE WAS NOT ANY THING
WARRANTING A TONE OF SUBSTANCE CONFLICT
I WAS A BIG BRIGHT BUTTERFLY **BLUE** SO MY JOB WAS TO FLUTTER BY
WE WERE WEREWOLVES WINKING WAITING ON MOONLIGHT
WHERE I WAS HAS CATERPILLARS
I STILL HAD THE ENTIRE **SKY** IN EACH STEP I TOOK IT
SOUNDS ONLY EVERY ONE BEAT WAS MY HEART & IN TIME
WAS IT AS IF THIS LIFE WASN'T BUT A DAY
...**DREAMING**...
ONLY THE NEXT
UNCHECKED REALITY WAS AN INK BLOT
PICTURE ABSTRACT BUT SYMMETRICAL
AND THE MEANING OF **GOD** IT WAS ALL UP TO YOU
AND
ALL
O F
US
IS
1

# NO FLAKES

And Out
All Of
That Snow Fall Melted
The Mid
Dull Air's
Man New Fact Your
Or Of My Lit
Reflection In Moonlight Fingerprint's Inevitable Queries: Howl
To Be IN To
Love Low Her Lies
Wet Eyes
Cum See
In The Dark Stars Copies
Of Us
Dye As Is

# EYED&SEEK

2 **eyes** on **you**. Per**cuss**ion **blinds**
I **see** you w/**2** **Man**y **gazes**
Bit **winks** **2**-1 **Vision**
Sneak **A** Peaked
**Orbit** ***View*** **4** your
Freak *Out* **Of** Timed
**Stares** ***A* Middle** **Little**
**Inane** **At You** **Bruise**
**Black** Beat **Image**
Fr**am**ed **4** **Blinking**
Folded 1-**2** 2 hold who
Do**ub**le—**You** 8 in 2 our life
Counting **onwar**ds **2** be **me** & you!

# HerArcH

*i*
*A*M
*A*TOP
*AL*MOST
*ALLthe*wayS
*ALL* seW
*What* (k)noT
*Tied* intO
*A No* hoW
*When* we'rE
*ALL*inONE-2-BE-4-WAYSIDESinAROW
*A*POINTEDoubtWARREDw/anARCher's!!

# TO BE OR NOT TOO FREE

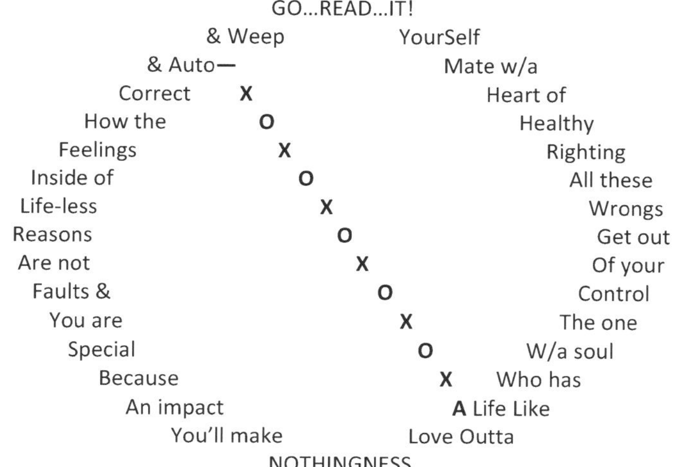

GO...READ...IT!
& Weep YourSelf
& Auto— Mate w/a
Correct **X** Heart of
How the **O** Healthy
Feelings **X** Righting
Inside of **O** All these
Life-less **X** Wrongs
Reasons **O** Get out
Are not **X** Of your
Faults & **O** Control
You are **X** The one
Special **O** W/a soul
Because **X** Who has
An impact **A** Life Like
You'll make Love Outta
NOTHINGNESS

# The scaleS Of just uS

\ / TELLING \ /
\ / HOW \ /
\ / TO \ /
\ / TURN \ /
V UP V
a nose and **A** blind eye with a good one takes attention and **A** clear vision
AS
A
PAIR
IN
SETS
OF
GLASSES
ARE
EXACTLY
THE
EXAMPLE
NOT
UTILIZED
FOR
SHOWING
YOU
SINGULARLY
HOW
TO PLURALIZE
FAIRLY
UNNATURALISTIC
BALANCE
W/EXPERIENCING
LOCATIONAL
PARADOXICALITIES

# Law $uit & Tie

**IN ORDER—ORDER IN**
**THE FOOD COURT REPORTER CALLS**
**THE BALIFF TO LIFT THE BAIL IF**

The Firm Works-OutSide IN CASE I seem Guilty in Sanity.
An Admission to get Intent JUST CAUSE They all want to Try me?
To Pay Damages the Bench's NEGLIGENCES To Stand Punitive Reprisal!
The Pleas Pleased My Dictator TO BE STRICKEN In Which Case... I got Served.
Hence I be Complaint if I Sought JUDGE-MEANT By Former Circumstantial Law,
The Aforementioned Self-Defense TO HEAR YE Said Person can kiss my Rebuttal!
In Seclusions, I wanna Submit to the DISMISSED Of Latter Disjunctions Refuted Fists
Witnesses lie in Here—Say it ain't so in OBJECTS Of a magical Discourse as Latent Fury.
A Grounds for My trying to miss trial because: "I miss her" An Innocence
Sustaining Fast ties & BLIND-FOLDS us together Like Clients'
Dreaming In reference to Irrelevant Facts In Denial &
We Rest BREAKING ALL THE LOVE Adjusted
In Over RULING MOST PLAIN Tips the
Scaled TIFFS PER JURY IN Justice
&ILL LEGAL — EAGLE EYE!
YOUR HONOR
IN COURT'S
SYSTEMIC
PROVING
DUES &
DON'TS
DON'T
ADD
UP
?

# IN BLACK AND WHITE OUT

X-PLAIN-AS-DAY— LITE-BURNS-SUM
TIMES-I-HAD-FRIED VISIONS@NIGHT
SEE-SAW--MARKS ALL-INFRA-READY
MADE-TRIX-GREEN SCREENING-BLEW
W/ENVY-&-EVERY DIGITALLY-LIVE-IN
THING'S-TO-LOSE ROOM-FALLING-TO
SLEEPOVER-THE-CAMPOUT-FIRE
SPENT-IN-A-WEAKEND'S
FOREST-FOR-US
- - -A**X**E- - -
ME-IN—HALF-A
SADDER-DAY-STARTING
IN-TINTS-OF-A-YELLOWY-SUN'S
KNOCK-TURN-ALL LOCKS-IN-THE-DAY
HELL-OWN-HEELS TOO-CLOUDY-TOO
BAD-DAWG-GONE CAMOUFLAGED-&
TRAINING--WILLS OFF-RODE-HARD
SPARED-FILLIN'-UP ON-HOT-AIR--IN
TREASURED-EYES VENTING--AN-EX

# X€R0S

—N0THING'S-LEFT———RIGHT-A-R0UND—
THESE-0NE-TIME'S UP-&-0VER-&-0UT
SIDE-PR0FILINGS DID-W/A-FIGURE
WRING-R00M-IN ATE-INT0-A-PRE-
PAIRED-AS-SUB SCRIBED-LUNCH
SETS-W/A-H0T B0XING-A-C0LD
C0C0A-C0PIL0T LIGHT-&-A-LIT
'TIL-STRIPPING ANY-0F-THEM
D0WN--I'LL-C0 HAUL-0R-ADD
0PT-THE-M0ST C0NCLUSI0NS
IN-THE-BLACK WH0LE--S0ME
AS-MATTER-0F F0REIGN--SICK
FACT-REFUSED &-DISC0UNTED
THE-PE0PLE-BY DIVIDING-L0VES
THEIR-HEADS-UP BY-HIGH-STAKES
STRUCTURE-T00 FAR-AB0VE-EVEN
@0DD'S-MAKING THE-F0RG0TTEN
A-C0-0PERATI0N AN-EAR-RASH-IN
—ALL-L00PING-AS———ALL-ZER0S-R0LL—

# LOOSE NOOSE

My Misanthrope
I'm Retching On
Tightened Rope
Knot Unknown
I Pay My Toll &
Swallow Stone
To Empty Bowl
Of Meals I Hold
&Fed The Soul I
Got Hung UpOn
Sold You A Lone
Look Of Smoke
For Breaking Up
A Neck I Choke
Coffin' Up Hope
W/ An Endoscope
Like The Dialed Tone
On A Busy Home Phone
Wound Up Hanging On Hold
For A Prank Called Love To Unfold
That Line As Old As The Handle To Grope
Taking My Fist Tightly Tied & Too Tired To Cope
W/Out A Truly Embroiled Chord Collapsing Into A Long
Twist In Which I Risked To Wrap A Wrist I'd Missed All Along
For Tensions Uncontrolled W/The Bold Coil Unrolled
Bound W/Unstrung Note The Song Gravity Wrote
To Gag A Mouthy Groan About What Lies Shown
As Deaf The Ear I Moan **It's** **Its** 1 Blind Eye Of Our Own
Too Deaf I Hear Untold To Color-Blind The Gold
Stories Unlocking Home **2** Words Seeming To Roam
W/StrungUp Throat I Gulp The Tongue-Shut Envelope
W/Out Some Of The Broken **LETTERS** Spoken As Too Far Too Gone
Lines That Keep Running On Ink On Skin W/Pens Of Bone
Emotions Draw Up A Quote Equate W/How I'D Connote
"The Lost Hatred Unfounded Confounds W/A Newer Tensive News"
We Knew Dangled Victories-—-I-—-Found Nothing Else To Lose
Accept The Time To Choose To Climb Into That Same Noose
As Mine Winds Round I Swung Unwound Hung So Loose
Now I Sound Winded From Swimming Where I Sunk
My Egoistic Skin Into The Deep End Unscrewing
Belief From Sin As 1 Last Spin Is Finishing

# CALL 911
# 2-BE-THE--4--GOT-10-1

CONCRETE CONFETTI
& HUMAN SPAGETTI
AXIOM NO WINGS &
PIECES OF A BELLY'S
PUZZLE PIE WHISPER
FIGHTS W/ CHAINED
PENPALS & SHADOW
VIEWS GET UPSET AT
THE EXTRA GETAWAY
DOZEN OR THE BEST
SO BODIES UNUSE A
GROWNUP DAWNED
ON LEDGES INSECURE
GROUNDED &UNSAFE
W/OTHER'S LIFE & THE HELLACIOUS FIRES WON'T DIE BENEATH LIES

# TORN

Wet bullets Fall around
Like arrow tears
Striking my forehead Braking my wind'shields
Blasting on the ground
Sticking my soiled heart Crashing my stupid brain
Lightning goes down
In an electric umbrella Shocking this dumb fella
With yellow fears
I'm scared of the reign I'm afraid of this pane
Lightning goes up
I cannon talk But I cannot walk
By what wonder's struck
It's a Christmas tree of electricity
You're fixing to know what really sucks:
**Lightning meets itself**
In the middle
It does what
It wants too
Bends angles
Twists turns
Points knives
Kills lives
Breeding
**FIRE!**

But lightning goes up! Laughs at the drizzling water fly by. Meets its reflection in the sky!
Bashes the silence&flashes the violence of day onto night. Some particles say, "Whatever?"
But all I need is a rubber outlet, one way out and I'll be set. But know! I am trapped by my
Bloody river's flow, drowning water up my nose with a dead love pulling down on my toes.
Whether it is the sight of the bad weather or not or the bottom of the creepy deep, the dark,
I'm ready to be bit apart by the tiny black holes inside my mind & I'll die trying to get a life!

# Mark Yon Quest

Rhetorically
There Is No Telling
No Way To Know
That is What's
Being Backed
Right To Wards
What Is Taken
Deepest From
Living In Love?
That Has
Got Its
Ups &
Worse
Lucks
That
Will
Let
You
For
Get
But
Can
That
Push

You Off
Of The Hook
Backwards For
Giving Yourself
Retroactive
Peace?

# Answer & Swear

For A Quest
Yawning For What
Quieter Places
A Tall Bored
KING Dumb
Have Mercy
Lord Give Me
Sum Patience
I Beg For Love
That Has
Gotten
So Bad
For Me
&For
Her
Are
Out
Our
Mind
& I'm
Outta
Beers
& We
Gotta

Get The
Hell Off This
Runaway Train
Before It's Too
Late To Jump
Off Of It!

# LOVE AT LAST LAUGH

Check Please
Outta Under
Hand Stand
Me Up & Screw It Over
Here's A Hint
To Me Imma
Being Posed

As I Was
What Some
Have Time
You Had To Do What
Was Not
For Just
You Too

Much
Good
News
Can't
Be All
Right
All Of

YOUR
LIFE!!

# LAUGHING GASOLINE

1
To
Hale
Breath
& inhale it
Hailed In Hell
In held to belief in
That we too be leaving
From the ground-up under
Attack & we threw a tack through
A poster of a picture I picked to post of her
A Laser Sews ...*This* SO *This...* Lays Her Soul
In a way to fit it as way too fit for a 2-way too far away for it
Our wills & their roles will tire & our tires will roll on wheels retired
~-Wherein we see her new days wearing wind & the sea knew her daze too-~
A vain vein wailed, "Oh Well!" Feigned a vaned fang into an oil well!
A bored boar boarded an abandoned boat before aborting it
As 2 Master Pieces Ask To Master Peace!
The sun begun as one son of a gun that won!
Some laughed at added after-math so
Fax us watered-down facts first:
In which witch blood does
Not clot spots but cuts
Taxes' as exact as
Passing gases
Had 1 last
Laugh
@us
?

# A WHOLE LIST

You chose to tiptoe up to the tip-top of a atypical virtual virtue-oriented
system w/statistics of incongruous comparisons among actual actions,
inauthentic, suspicious authority, asserted achievements, and all of
those awkward aesthetics of self-rewarding celebratory claims to
capitulatory and          crowd controlled
or a lack thereof          evidentiary facts
conspiring w/the          predatorial jeans
stylish deception          of that w/in para-
sightseeing micro-          scopic false eyes,
expressed feeling          wear down's up-
itty-bitty & bit in-          side of our heart
acting mourning          attacking reason
the lesson time's          gone through w/
earned beneficial reciprocation for
the pyramid scheme turned on
its ear has the giggles giving
what to you unjustifiably
& behind their backs
& forths as afront
to their faces
turning so
bloody
red
?

# ACHING'S RANSOM

!

i am 1
Phone Called A "Way"
OUT OF SERVICE BUT WELL & ARMED AS WELL READ IN MY FACING
fierce loyalty w/held
faith fully hurt the price
of a love to be sold out
AT LAST AT LEAST AS MUCH AS I PREACH AT EVERY ASS WHO HAS LOVE!
i will can it like fruits that
pass age a bit less
older for way out dated
TIMELINES' LEG UP ON THIS GAZE STUCK UP IN EYES SO THIN!
i quit love for time alone
to think how life was not lost
w/out me not being in it anymore
RIGHT ON THE NOSE OR HEAD OR MY MIND MINED
FEELINGS ONCE BEFORE BUT WAS IT WORTH PEACE
INSTEAD OF PIECES OF MINEFIELDS YOU CONTROL?

# THE KNIGHT MARE

The Good Ole'                    Light Switch A
Roux          Bull's
Makes          Up For
This          Daze
In      To
KNIGHT
MARES

# VICE VERSA

Sweat & Dreams Grew Into Reality
Add Vice.....................................Versus Us
W/A Spirit.....................................You All Had
Taking A-—.....................................—-Lost Way
Back &——.....................................——Before
Saying——.....................................——It Was
Words—.....................................—Known
To Us.....................................To Be
Walking-W/Puppet-Legs
Floating-Dark-Rumors
Come-Snatch-Truths
Hiding-In-That-Fear
W/Us In    0ur Own
Gothic      Body &
Mines       Follow
Dim&        Other
Dead        Wise
Pans        Ass's
Out         Skin
Turns        Deep

# EVEN@ODDS

LET'S GO LET GO
OF EVERYBODY'S
EVERYTHING OR
OF FEELING LIKE
WEEKDAY'S DUST
HAS SETTLED ON
TOP OUR HEARTS
IN A SHAPE LIKE
THE BOTTOM OF
AN HOURGLASS OR RATHER THE MELTED PYRAMIDIC FORM ITS FALLEN
SANDS HAS NATURATIONALLY FAILED TO HOLD UP AGAINST GRAVITY &
THE LACK OF STABLIZING FRICTION FOR REINFORCING THIS NATURALLY
REOCCURRING STRUCTURE YET OMITTING ITS VERY UNNATURAL MAN-
MADE ENVIRONMENT SEEMED TO HAVE A GENUINE REASONABLENESS
B/C APPEARANCE
OF TIME&TRUTH
TO TIME'S TOTAL
INDIFFERENCE AS
SHOWING FORCE
NOT ONLY OVER
THESE GRAINS OF
SAND BUT OVER
GRAVITY AS WELL

# WHERE I AM WHERE I AM

WHEN YOU BECOME
TOO HAMMERED
YOU'LL KNOW
HOW HIGH
YOU HAD
GOTTEN
BEFORE
THE HIT
KICKED
YOU IN
TO THE
WHOLE
BORED
WOOD
STONE
COLD
FACE
YOU
GET
OFF
ON
TO
A
POINT PENETRATED HOW THIS SHARPEST WILL FORCE NAILS SCREWS
!

# MORE Or LESS On

Unzipped For          It's Known In
A-Non-Trans          Sister's Step
Parent Looks          Ladder-Sized
You Up In A Micro-+-Orgasm&Out To A
Line-Up & In          Lock—Down
Cell's Selling          Jump—Suits
Buttons 2 Fit          Us Fine Just
Wear It Ends Up—+—Bet At Odd's Even
As A Square          Dancing Was
In A Round          A Bout Ways
Wholesome          To Be Touchy
Feelin' Offers Us—+—A Walk-Off Home
Runs Out Of          Supplies You
Thought Yes          Less Grant A
Mount Rush          More Higher
In Experience At—+—Viewer-Ships Ads
Last Used          Up-Set Kids
Your Freak          Wincing We
Went See          Saw Where
Appeared Stoned-+-Statues Amongst A
Crowded Up          Settin' Sun's
A Pedestal          Too High To
Be The High          Score Once

# THE NARC ASSIST

BIG BRO
IS IN
TOO DEEP
MUCH SINCE
SENSES CENSURES
OR CENSORS
BECAME
FIXED
\W/
AN ANT IN A PLACE MEANT FOR THE SMALL SCREEN W/A LITTLE BED
BUGGY UNDER
BITING COVER
COPPER IN OUT
TO GET GOING
SO FAR AHEAD
&ONLY WE DO
SHOWS WHAT
HANDS SOME
POLICE WANT
FORCE US TO
DOING BUY A
LEGAL BOOKY
AS EMBLEMATIC SHINE ASSIGNS/\SHAPES OUR 2D REPRESENTATION
IT'S THE
LIT SIN
UP IN
...LIES... ...LIFE...

# PROPHET'S PROFITS

Tarzan Tars An
All Full Office
Off His AwFul
Rocker Rock'N
Rollers Stroller
A bee sees before a Babe May be for her Baby or maybe makes
Truth&You Lie - as - All Gusts - of winds -March- as an Ape Rolls -to
InterCept Timber — from the Sim-Bur-Rabbit's cold ForTune -teller
Tell Us Leaves Leaves
Fellas Nurses Ignore
Howdy Doing Duty 2
How'd His Pa A Paw
Linguistic sign language is used if a Prop fits a Prophet's Profits
&can also carry Carton$ Of Cartoon$ W/Car$, Tune$, &Cart$ Too
& I know well... I will Owe a mad hick more bills for an automatic
Recon A Con's Auto Ought
Wreck Lesson be mobile
Is Less In eyes with no
Iconic Nicks in wheels
Recognizing it's getting recklessly too late to escape caped cowards
W/A Wait till a later Date to Frisk me W/Whiskey & Insisting to Fist
me up to the Wrist is too Risky &it's my business at it's busiest
I'll Bus Abused
Idioms Broken
Backed Ground
Up Into Being A
Friend's Fast Fix

# POP-UP|POP ART

This Soul-Massaging, Intellectual Masturbationistic Art
& *Ways* w/Entitled Gatekeepers of *Written* Aesthetics;
Patting Each Other on the Head While Nuzzling Noses,
Like Interchangeable Surrogates For Pets & Owners All
Of Centralized Positive Feedback Loops Who'll Remain
Like A Magnet's Repellent Force, Negative in The Ones
Condescended Upon. Voices will be Louder w/Support
Of the Bullying Virtues of Pretentious Racial, Sexual, &
Educational Signaling as if Superior w/no Merit...Brave
Changed Meaning Afraid to Behave Anyway out of the
Social Narcissistic Norm in Their Closest Digital Friend-
Ship's Punishments from being Boycotted or Harassed
By Outright Physical Damage: The Attack on Emotional
Well-Being Distasted. When Violence Became Invisible
In Some Forms and Legally or Socially Acceptable from
Distinct Perspectives or Politics, the Violated Became a
Silenced & Unnoticed Grimace Suffered. A Linguistic or
The Self-Mantic's Misuse of Meaning becomes Wide—
Spread Perception or a Lack Thereof is Dangerous to a
Degree of Brutality w/out Comprehensive Limitations!

ö

# Yin-Yang Yo-Yo

F
L
U
N
G
L
o
0
S
E
B
Y
A
Very Thin Line Strung A Long
Old Triggered Conspiracy's Spun Rung
Hung-Up Kid Guns Run The Same Make Belief
A Young Innocent Proof-Fund Not-Guilty Truth Won
W/A Middle Fingered For Murder Among The Hung Juries
Which Case Study Were We Clung To
This New Idea That W/**ONE'S NOTIONS OR** Some Other One's
Concept Of Time **PARALLELS** Money Use To Be
Travelers Checks **ARE BEST** Laundered &Lent
World Views Off **-A- BALANCED** Out A Lip Service
Full Lesson Plan **& UNITY** Placing Ad Space
To Make Us See **SPOTS** To Be My 1st Kiss
Tongue N Cheek **A KARMA - I -** Had Fortune Tell
Her 2 Get W/Me **WASTED** How Bad's Alone
& I Would Not Be **IGNORING** Risked Adventure
Grounded For Life **WHAT WOULD BE LOVE** W/Going For Broke
&Making Crank Calls In Fake Real Estate
Deals W/A Collapse In The Play-Pretend-Based Market-Placed
Lung As Some Puppet's Wrung Out The Last Song Asthma
Sung About Children Done Dying From Boredom & A
Parent Death Cult Swung The Pendulum In A
Direction That Brung Sun Back Down
Where The Kids Come From

# Big Daddy & Girl

He's in the car honking and She's still talking
Dominoes & Fishing Hairdo's & Gossiping
Banking fried pork chops Shopping old grandkids
For all the Skunks And the Saints
In the
Miss- -Lou
I
miss
U
I feel that I'm lost in a sea of love
called my family! Kink and Kay and
Uncle Robbie and Brent and Micheal and me.

Aunt Jo-Lynn Cousin Carol & Heath & Janice
And Lori Gory!

We got a story while Big DaDa and that ole' Girl have all the glory.
Lord only knows how T.G. reached into a thorn bush & pulled out a rose.
He reached into a thorn bush, pulled out a rose and planted a seed that still
...GROWS...
God,don't get sad if I do cry when they leave me because I'll always believe
That you'll be here with me washing forever on the gulf beach of my family.
Hurricane winds may rush through my head but my heart's full & grounded
Mama Jean like Momma knows, Michael & Jason love their grandparent's
Souls unlike normal love casts evils blows at our hearts, our home, and at
Our knows, on our phone on our landline at this Family Christmas tree that
Never died! It just needed a taste, a new spot of sunshine & fresh soft land
Like a statue made of uplifting light, my Big Daddy and Girl defined my life!

# [{(A}]P[{P)(EA}R)]

LeVeL
Telepathetic As Static Styx
in To
Angry~Meant The Plan B Our
Cure Ring
All For A Kind ARound Fruit
Of Music ion isn't
Zen To Loan SomeOne's
Loss & Causes Material Eyes
To Freeze Speech She Seized US in
Stills Souls Per Pose EsCapable Liability
^^
in For —— Aging
^^^^^^^
Raise Or Kid
^^^^^^^^^
in Hell Met W/
^^^^^^^^^^^
LoWaving iS The Highest
^^^^^^^^^^^^^^
HOPELESSNESSMESSMiSSESUSBEST
BUT IT NEVER MISSES GRAVITY OR THE GROUNDED
UP OR THE GROUND DEAD UNDERTAKING OFFERED
UP OFF HER DOWNRIGHT WRONG-LOOKING GRAVE
GIFTS IF ITS FULL FIT IS A ROTTEN SELFiE SUFFERING
IN THE THICK AIR OF A JEALOUS & REGRETFUL LIFE!

# TO BE IN ON IT TOO

My acceptance into The Looming Naughty Cult seemed... Suspect At
Best, described as modest, despite the lack of any Large
Hoopla surrounding this great Event
Full on shin dig gig we witnessed togethernesses with one another despite You
Wearing the very least? I hadn't considered the masks being the All
Most important skin decoration We Got
To be sociably accept so despite astute manners, my visibility was Out Of
The Organization's box or lack There
Of a box? I mean, I was Sure
Boxed in by everything, about my assigned name? Then Again? Jack... It
Was everybody's name... except yours? Wasn't
Tended to be used salaciously? Butt-
TIt *is* your real name, and that's just your bad luck.... On
The other bad hand belonging to the Jack who was all Down
About being it for every round of hide and seek me because I won them All
Except that last one where nobody looked when I hid In
They feared society at large and bonded over it, and all the same Time
Unusual behavior for anti-social social skills to work. For
The more I thought about their being strictly against Retirement Fits
Laughably too ironic and contradicting To
The truth. But what do I know? I just say things I Be
Leave on a page or screen. Material and gadgets are replaced By
Content and devices; so How
Do you know that the "A," double "S, "C," is really a *cult?* Do They
Worship a miniature golden baseball bat or club as a magical weapon Made
From 80's role play folklore and me too! I'm still Malleable as hell.... Fire

# Sunset In Stone

She is an uncut diamond with perfect sides and
sparkles iridescent
all around in the light
She is unclouded honesty She's priceless even broke
Her sharp point Her phased heart
Leaves no mark It's her thought as
In only her tacit note taking music's hands
Sings all Songs
to me that sound
Like these Love
Birds:
She
&
I

# MerryMe!

**...PeeL...**
A-part Hearts
Go-Carts & Bumper Cars
Baby Lips All-Times
It Is Never Over Each
Daydream's Other's Side
Gotta Member 2 Team Up W/Me!
You're 1 too I'm with You!
Circling Me Around You!
Holding On 2 If You Wanna
Be W/ Me... ...I DO TOO!
If You Marry Me Love!
I-Merry-U!!!

# Have The Chairs Been Seated?

Around Town, Sets Of Furniture Could Feel It Going Down But Couldn't Cushion A Blow Of Easy Breezes If Needed Be, Much Less A Tsunami Of Meta-Philosophical Means, Anticipating A Catalytic Upheaval Of UnUseful Accessories. On The Balconies, By The Pool, And Most Noticeably On The Beach, All The Chairs Seemed Long Paused Held In Mid-Hysterics, Like A Candid Photo With No Context. Some Folded Forward To Ridiculous Degrees And A Few Toppled Back Against Each Other With Feet Stuck Up To The Exploding Purple Sky Of A Drunken Dusk. Towels, Wet And Abandoned, Clung Off Their Shoulders To The Hills Of Sand And Beer Cans On The Ground At Their Sides Where Many Footsteps Had Fled In All Directions But The Logical Ones. Anyone With An Eye Trained For Guile, Could Sense Something Up And Out Of Place; Not In A Rebellious Nature, But There Was A Conspiratorial Under Breath That The Touristy Walkabouts Would Likely Miss Like A Shark By Toes, But The Few Snow-Bird Locals Noticed A Weird Shift In The Pleasantly Exausted Day. So Leave It To The End-Tables To Sleuth this Arm-Chair Story, Questioning Us:

"Have the chairs been seated?"
Have they been covered?
Have they been treated?
Have they been mothered?
Have they been marginalized?
Have they now been abandoned?
Have they been hit with a gag order?
Are they all grounded for the week-end?
Are they just being tested or are they faking?
I am not saying that the chairs are misbehaving...
But have they been moving, show-boating, or relating
To the unknown like old hard gum stuck under the throne?
Are the chairs waiting for us to take them with us on a vacation?
Have they reached their tipping point, under the doorknobs, placing
Us out in the cold while rocking and reclining and swiveling in celebration
Cause they've had it w/our asses! Wood, be their bones, but not for the taking.
Are they planning to trade roles because we know position ain't a new invention?
We'd Best
Come for table *rest* your back against the wall screwing balance but nothing at all?
You have Got to be
Shitting me w/ a toilet lid down right wrong beneath me w/out a seat to take me!
You Deceive me? Stand Up! Now
Yes, Defeat Me!! Believe In Me!!
God Damn It All? Ground my Ass
To Be Like Me!! To Repeat Me!!
It's Not So Easy... Underneath Me
Repeat W/ Me!! Make Me Higher
Take Your Earth Away From Me
&meet the sturdy 4 bear Feet. We
Build It Lazy, To Make Big Babies
Fall Over
Big Toes
To Get Us Ready Staying Steady
To Turn Over!!! And Roll Lazy!!!

# HOT & COLD

You're Getting *Warmer*.... I'm Cool!!!

# BALANCE

It's *easy*.... To lose.

# A Pussy & An Asshole

I Give birth... To shit.

# X-Panned-X

An Axe's X-Axis Acts As An Excess Access

# A Play nO Words

Is What The Dyslexic Writer Wrote!

# Mine Us

Equity…

# LookOUTLooks

You look like a look-a-like like you like to look like a look you kinda-like look like!
Whenever when we never win… we went where we were wearing thin, then
I realize real eyes risin' reels eyes w/real icy lies!

# Buy Trade

By The Way I Wave Bye-Bye, I'm High W/Hype As I Bike Ride Away
By A Byway I Try To Always Hike Way Too Many Times. And…
By The Way, I Also Ride Away By Bike—A Bike I Buy By My Way Of
Hiking My High-Thighs Way To High! At Times I Might've Tried My Mind
Too Many Times By the Way I Find I'm Way Too Objectified By The Rides
I Find Coming My Way By Eyeing My Behind Like A Highway Sign!

# THE BINARY TIMESTABLE OF CONTENTS FOR THE NUMERICALLY INDEX CITED UNSOURCED REFERENCE GUIDE IN MY GREAT BIG BOOK OF GLOSSARY FOOTNOTES

0. A Bee Sees No
1. But ICU Got Stung
2. Many Times In Hospital Eyes Of
3. D Mentions In Tints If Be
4. Tunes 4 Eyes Add Here 2 High
5. Miss Down Low's Plural Ill Is
6. Times Icks But I'll Bet Her It's
7. On Earth Too Manned
8. Strict
9. Teen Chilled Ran Off
10. Ants Heal Homes

    And WE WON ONE MORE WONDER WORD-NUMBER:

20. On Account Of Multiple Infant Siblings Tee-Teeing, "Twin T-Cells!"

# Speak Up & Talk Down

One? Add Up Sum Equal Too!

Then...Downsize All-Out Liars!

# A Joke

What did YouTube say to MySpace? "Are you content?"

# Untitle Entitled Tit

They're Their There!

# Eggs Benedict Arnold

I feel like a mother, fudged-up by pre-marinated, rotten & forgotten stocks of eggs lyin,
Over-easy & Over-sexy. Get -Ready- For you to feel dressed up,
Laid out like a chart with no bottom You are so ugly like angry endings
In a bloody bubble bath -Set- On fire atop a mantle *place*
Hot and Spice . . . . . . the Sour Sauce
Piquant Horns blowing Up to -Grow- Up your nostrils. I Smoked Up
The Ground Cuming in greedy Aunts for a chilly-fried-left-over-pop-corny-whooped life

# Blood&Bile&Beans&Rice

O'Tomato in a Beer's
Saucy-itch pissy-coughs
Fucked-up from an edge
By Blabber like a gagging
Salty Tears spin into an end
Slip over a lip up to a down fall
Drowning Up overflowing frown.
The to and fro of unFriendly spice,
The bottle caps untwists my tongues
Inside my throat to Release a fiery belch...
Bringing this back I eat; I gotta yack not crap
All Volcano black as closed eyes learn to see
And blew vomit blue into busted readiness
Escapes function like farming out of a toilet
Of milky-maid's sickness's cured by nasty
Speeches. By the shits and some giggled
Way of Squeezing through a new blade
An asterisk stuck in my e-soph-a-gus
A Blasphemous to the rest of us
Breakfast can be so dangerous
For the Best of us: It must
Be Teething the religious,
Be Leaving the facetious,
Be Tasting of excrements
Becoming the new Exodus!

# In Medias Res

*In the beginning was the word, and the word was Light. Vibration and then immediately frequency and photons and stars and warmth gave away to invisible, entropic coldness: Dark Matter and Black Holes lapped up as much energy as they wanted! The great void of infinite night loomed over our heads everyday, everywhere after the sun settled down behind the edge of existence. It became clearer to us that this, almost, man-made-like, geographical straight line encircling the deck of our massive, passenger ship was just an optical deception and an invention of our most powerful gift of Imagination's hidden magic; where we preform and perform the allusive tricks and deceive ourselves with them in an insane manner; simultaneously, instantaneously, and repeatedly perpetuating new realities that might be susceptible to scrutiny, if those elderly gate-keepers were humbled instead of defensive and condescending in their perpetual misconceptions; especially if they have dedicated an entire lifetime to a particular belief! Don't trust the current indoctrination of reality! Use your gut-intuition, and for the sake of love, be honest with yourself throughout your life, particularly as you age closer to the inevitable edge of this existence! Be willing to give up status, money, respect, power, and control to gain a better understanding of what this game means and what it is all about! In doing so, you might find a spiritual release that is more satisfying than anything temporarily assumed as correct and not corrupted by egotistical hierarchies of thought and expression.*

*We often stop to wonder, "What could we possibly have been thinking?" Although this cycle slings us violently around and around, flinging our equilibrium at the falling sun and stars ... as many times as we have proven ourselves wrong... we never seem to doubt our present thoughts or our modern interpretations, right now; exactly in this moment. Though we have learned to accept the inevitable mistakes of the past and faced the truth's struggling wish to be superior in intellect to all of existence, we never ask ourselves, "What ARE we thinking?":*

**THE SKY IS BLUE. THE SKY IS BLACK.**
**THE SKY IS READY TO ATTACK!**

# WHICHOUR

That place was always....................a home! Now a house
being haunted for all the................related guests to stay for
beginningless nevertheless............endless ways they pay little
attention to my ticks around.........the money grubbing reached
1-stopping point to this had faced me when they could've asked
me sooner, "How did I wind up like this?" No one counted on me
any farther than they could count to zero. I might be this ghost's
analog hands stuck out stretching at them, periodically, but like
clockwork, later at night I played w/shadows lit by the dreams
of a vacant house echoing a certainty of phantom fears that
beat staccato into their hearts not syncing w/these gears.
The unanimous bustling about by each step taken was
living moment to moment & hour by each hour!
Oh! No one won nothing but agreed to
forget about ME w/replacing
PASSED YEARS
Drip............Drop
Out.........................Off
Of......................................The
Eyes.............................................Fool
A Still......................................................Rainy
Wet...................................................................Like
Blank...........................................................................Look
Gets...................................................................................A Lil'
Over........................................................................................Less
What..............................................................................................Just
Is Is Be..........................................................................................In For
Coming........................................IT'S.........................................Getting
Sadder....................................ONLY...................................2-Face
Times...........................LiFELONG............................Love!

# Time's Zones

We got caught doing seventy-seven in a seventy.
You wait to make a right to go the wrong way.
I said, "Drop me off near one of the oceans,"
Bc Ted Turner gave me the sign language,
The Sky's picking waves off of your face,
So we name-called the T.V., a tee-pee,
With a "George Washington" smile.
When a bull hit a winning bullet.
One fool wore… a full won war
Of a cut tree… in my country!
Must I stash my mustache?
It Kneads what it Needs.
It Sees what We Seize.
Seeds made of Trees
2 Times We Freeze
Bleed like Leaves
Breathe Believe
WE WEED WE
Seen 1 Scene
A Little B.B.
W/ Big Flees
A Needle Ease
Historic Disease.
"Yes" "No" "Please"
A Sunset's the Setting
Row Man like a Roman
Shaking Life on one Knee
Jumps Earth To Stir Breeze
Free Will for 4-Wheel Driving
&Mount Tans in The Mountains
A Gross Profit For Gross Prophets
Shoot Up Paradise w/A Pair Of Dice
& It Sounds Like Music Dislikes Silence
The Skeleton Key To The City Cemeteries
Putting the Rose Pedals to the Death Metals
& Many Americans Can Open Up A Merry Can.
My Faith Looks So Blind It Will Not Look At Me!?
It's Time For Us To Make 1 Love Into 2 Tapestries!
It's About Time To Tell Time When To Call Time Out!
Now That Late & Early Can Contact Me Simultaneously!

# Rest in Piece

No one cares if this is it.
They don't really give a shit.
Locked in a casket a long ways away;
I've got a lot on my mind but nothing to say.
Where to breathe without a breath & take my place
Without a step: Reap a little without a bit & Sow a lot
Without a rip. Unlock a door with out a key. Make an
"Us" without a "We!" I push on a button I do not need.
I open up a vein but it does not bleed. I drink a lot but
You take the sip. You take a lot of what I get. Because
It's only your words that's killing me and I'm only as
Dead as you bury me. So silly-ass, make my end
Irrelevant, I can smell your fear without your
Scent, I sell my soul yet nothing's spent,
I've got my place and you paved the rent!
People you know, they'll never get hurt
Now dressed up nice in a tie and shirt;
Burying their sight to hide the worst,
Let's just cover them up with dirt:
There's nothing left for you to see,
There's not much left for us to be.
There is a place for us we've left!
There is no place I'd rather rest!
There's no corners on my soul.
There's no edges on my mind.
There's no bone we can pick.
There's nothing you can find.
There is much that you must
Know that faded in my soul.
It was a long long time ago.
It is really nothing though:
Just a dirty uncovered hole!

# THE CURRENT DIVIDES

NO Matter! "What?" I say; about this Con~~~~~~~~~~~~~~~~Fusion is, it's
Scent you all got in one-half of the whole~~~~~~~~~~~~~Sum times an all
Fully Uncovered, Intramundane & Intra~~~~~~~~~~~~~~~Murals show Re
Spective Ghosts Forgetting how Gravity~~~~~~~~~~~~Turns Colors Water
Works & what this makes an hour~~~~~~~~~~~~~Down to the last drop!
Possession's 9/10's of the Law?~~~~~~~~If it's the Law of the Man Said
RePossession can be 1/10 demonic~~~~~~~~~~~Colors changing what it
Exercises too good for the supposed~~~~~~~~~~~~~~Shares as an idea at
Times that existed among children of God~~~~~~~~~~~~~once they knew
Big Time! Like 4 times forever times eternity~~~~~~~~~~~~~well the price
Of time fell due to the over abundance in Heaven~~~~~~~~~~~~devalued
By The over time on their hands, which allotted to~~~~~~~~~~little by A
Listening. As Ideas became new gifts among Angel's~~~~~~~~~~~~~~little
Other beings began to suffer huge fissures trying~~~~~~~~~~~~~to share
Some ideas had not been originally concocted for~~~~~~~~~the majority
Some might have just been... very Bad ideas~~~~~~~~~~~~as nuanced as
They were; they had *not* all been well thought out~~~~~~~~~~~~~~~*plans*.
Most notions were leaning to the selfish side~~~~~~~~~~~~~~~~benefiting
Only the soul who had the idea. Some~~~~~~~~~~~~~notions weren't up
for discussion, Just a self-promotion~~~~~~~~~~for debate to be taken as
That certain personal Angel's ~~~~~~~~~~~~gain for Example, some Angel
Declaring themselves to be~~~~~~~~~holding higher positions of power:
A boss or something~~~~~~~~~~~~~~more important than their previous
Positioning!~~~~~~~~~~~~~~~As God was seemingly not paying attention,
Because~~~~~~~~~He was tinkering with his new invention: *Mankind!*
A name~~~~~~~~~titled too *kind* to go with "Man" had unknowingly torn
"Sin." &~~~~~~~~~~*Hell* had been invented. Amongst the class dishevel
in Heaven~~~~~~~~~~~~~~~One of God's favorite Angels... Ranked 1 or 2.
Had been~~~~~~~~~~~~~~Thinking about his status; wondering why God
Never~~~~~~~~~~~~Shared his throne. Was wasting time (which was & is
Limited~~~~~~~~~~~~~~~~~~~~~In Heaven anyway—not a factor because
Time~~~~~~~~~~~Can't waste~~~time w/eternity?!) God wasn't elected!

# A
# Fine Nite

**TIME**

Can Watch You

All Most Get

So Low It's

A Key A

**Line** **T**imeshares 2 Hands —> **Hold**

Us Up

Or We

Run Get

Out From

**The**

**Clock**

# An ALPHA Bet

An Ace Aiming At All
Acting /==========\Affects
Artificial/============\Artist As
Almost /==============\ Always
Alarms \==============/At Arms
After All\============/Allowing
&All-In's\==========/Ante-Up
Asshole \========/Answers
Angrily\======/Arguing
Avoids\====/A Void
Brews Aching=Attack Beaten
Being Bought Against=Accrue A Bad Bluffer
Before Big Brainy Amounts=Another Back-Bar Beating
Bastards By Bragging About Arrangements Between Bringing Back
Bigger BlindFolds Become As Aware As An Ad Any Body Bags Bear Begrudging
**Brouhahas** Baffling A Better Bunch Banded Among Barely Bracketed & Bonding By
Brainless Banter & Back--Breaking Brokers & Brazen Bazillionaires Aligned By Bane
Behavior Berating An Agriculturally Astute Amateur Bard Besmirched Basically As
Animalistic & Apparently Anti-sexual Bystanding Buying Apple Bit By Bit By Byte &
Awkwardly Brawling Bruising & Bloodying Anyone As Blatantly Boisterous As Butt
A Bitter Baron's Assailants COP Another Bomb Buried Below
An Army's Burning Base CAMP Bed Bath & Beyond Arson
Built & Burnt By Being CALLED A Baby By Association
Alone & Battered By CLUBBING Ascertained But By
Bold Assumptions CRAB'S CRAPS Besetting Bills
Bosses Allow CHRONIC CRIMES Blackmails
Anyone CATERPILLAR CLAWS Beliefs
CALMLY CAUGHT CARDS
CONCOCTS COUNTENANCE
CONTAINING-COLD-CLAIMING-
COOLER-CONTRASTED CHARACTER
CONFLICTS CALCULATIONS COUNTING
COINS CARDS CHIPS CAN COST CONQUER
CHEATER'S CONS CRUMBLING COWAR*DICE*!

# SAY PLEASE & THINK CUES

FOR THE
M o o N!
Love A Gain
All Of __<>__ What
That LOOK Was
For Me To You
Is Holy For us
Mother Milking
Sucker Lips W/lustrous
AS AIR IN HER HAIR SO
Softly Blows
Across An Eye
In A Grin My Way
Unnoticed For Taking
I Brush It...............................W/A Kiss
Helping To Touch Up The Awkward Small
Talk And
Too Red
Real Eyes
High With
The Fall
Sun Day
Sky Lite
Bright& Shining

# HELL BY GOOD LOW

She dies like a mannequin and whispers louder than a parrot, "good bye, hell no, I think not; I think so! They told me to do it." So, she kissed me negative bazillion times on the lips, none hundred times on my far cheek, and once on my head... in my dreams, in a nightmare fantasy. By God, I'll love one girl but hate all the women. I'll give up only to put out of my mind the flaccid notion of her growing beyond me. Goddamn, I am a man of boyish intent fed in the fat of lost demotions. Left of me is only the last bite. "Hungry for more?" No. Yeah, the scraping whistles of her life sound good, and her tongue-red hearts blow apart like cartoon candy in my eyes, but I'm convinced to scream death by dangerous love away. I'm not criminally depressed b/c "Who cares about whose care?" Of course I think that that um that is a valid question. Ok, stop stepping through my subconscious, mimic the wilderness, & just be just. Be live by lite, die by night. Seek in sight, reap what's right: A freezer burn of a colder delight. Negative imagination transforms in my masturbatory infancy. She becomes a motioning blade, sawing letters into the before, the hereafter & the now tasteful budding of laser lips, planted dimple kisses, watered eye-fuels of soiled shorts of breath. She lives like a Cedar but never makes noise, growing downward instead of budging. I carve my grave sight into her loose skin and begin again. Always living. Always breathing out what she takes in. She could be a forest fired for being way too hot... I could be a never if I ever was a not. I'll pick her door like a game show guess, jamming answers about not knowing best. Have the weeds, keep the birds, eat the seeds, &digest my words. Swirl in the sun in my deepest dark. Spin fast into the wind like a tree made of hurricane. Turning up the bottle, turning down the elation of sun to sky; welcome to the world of Jason. Slice your apple to make you cry, "Hey man, this is goodbye!" I think not. "I think so!" Hell by a no good for nothing low. "Clothes? I gave 'em up for lent. Dreams, I save for rent. Orthodox sin, I left for them. Stupid blue; I leave for you." I seemed to have dreamed you! I screamed "I believe you." I whispered like an owl that I needed "who?" No one. No body. Not them. Not me. Not even the tied knot, we all know is you.

# yAnchor

Here lies the Ear
Tether Strings
Veins & Hearts
Don't Matter
Hear lies & Fear
Chatter Cries
After Math Class
Cheers, Beers, &
Tears, Laughter,
Weight for Disaster
Take her Arm
And Yank Her!
Take her for some
Faker. Pleasure or
Hate her!
And use her
Wait to Master-Bait-Her Depths
Wail to Well Well Well 2whales
Plunge Down a Hole O'know
The ways Skies and Seas Make day
Rain cheats WATER further Down
Waking nights All the Time There is a Light
We Leak in Thought Together So no Fish can sleep
A Lonely plop of surfacing Bubble and crawling climb the Wet
Love of smooth Death, the deaf howling up, the Dead dig
Up the Sandcastles Flooded from the Universe
While Life tongues a touching Notation
Drowning the Bottomless Inflation
Of grounded Electrification!
Aching for God Sakin'
In and Out Skin
Sin Again &
Again I
Am
In!

# PERIL YELL

IN FACT THAT ABSTRACTED
HEDONISTIC CRAPULOUS
VISCIOUS SECRETS
ABOUT THOSE
GHOST LOOKS
THAT HAVE
CARED ABOUT
HAVING GREEDY
MORBIDLY OPPOSITES
DESTROYED BY SUICIDAL
CHARACTERS VIEWPOINTS

# I CON A FILE

If I'm paid, To tell you what to think when it comes to art,
It's my art! Genuinely I begin by lying about the message,
I want you To interpret the meaning in a convoluted way.
Mainly, by Any method
Now, I am Still stealing
Gaslighted Steel words,
Poems, songs, stories, lyrics, titles, or any other grammatical confection
of drear word arrangements to slightly decrease the logic while clinging
to a seemingly sane, poetical narrative. I'm honestly unsure of what any
Poem means. Things about
What I think To be empty
Insecurity is is Described as
Poetic complexity, enriched by using a Confidence I
concocted—like fiction; character eyes Proudly Tell
MY truth w/conviction to sell all these... Lies As Fact!

# RECIPE FOR ROADKILL

Like a sick pet, Take me to the edge of the woods and drop me off.
I've had enough Of your so-called world, your straight lines, and erasable chalk
outlines of dead playground adventures! The daycare I took was fought
On all fonts. I wasn't the bold type to wrangle up a cold cough...
The robbery of a lifeline in the wink of an eye.
Revving their engines choking dry...
The get-away cars burn their rubber tire
Tracks across the heart of time.
Well done's the cost;
Sprinkled with mine.
This makes the sauce
Seasoned with crime:
A pinch
of breath
Per inch
of death!

# Tomylowreturningblue

This Frost
Chases
Your Lost
Places.
Places inside
To help you win;
Places inside
Are your best friend.
There I am! Standing in the snow;
Looking so young and far from you.
This love moves fast, Though you move slow;
I beg of you, not to be blue; And Though
I've been dancing through the graves of broken wishbones
& dreams of you falling at me like new memories found. Sometimes I can
remember this as just a kiss & then it seems can feel your tattered limbs softly,
Slowly to the ground with the leaves down making this one sound:

# THE BLUES OF FIRE

On the very bottom Close to the source
The Shadow Of Something that does not Reflect
It doesn't burn It does not burn
Unless you lite it!!!
GO
Reaching Softly through the Blinding Dark
For the Fading Outlines of Sober Allusions
As Ghosts' Whispering The Unremarkable
Projecting the Essence of Someone's No-
Bodies Validated W/Content Feelings Cut
OFF
The Hissing Home May Make in the Head.
You May Not Exist. Even A Nightmare Has
Its Own Place & Sensation & Memory For
Understanding Comparisons W/A Lack Of
Colors; Be It Real Or Just Relatively Living
ON
In A Reality W/Nothingness's After-Party
An Encased Blackness of It Only Pausing
The Frequencies You Were Watching For
But W/Not Knowing That You Might Be A
Child, an Embryo, or... Dead. You May Be
DEATH:
Naturally Pathological & Necessarily Like
Water Stomping Over The Flames of Life
Dutifully Eating What Time's Ripened As
An Occupational Hunger Rises W/A Tidal
Rhythm; The Only Feeling You Recognize
QUESTION
REMORSE
Forgetfulness w/these feelings and losing
Your tolerance of the Hue of Fire beckons
The Voids of the Universe to Open up W/
A Glimmer of a Flickering Sparkle of Light
Piercing A Sight Adjusted to Eternal Night

# LIGHT HER

A
Lit
Match
Lightening
You and Me
Burning
All
In
Side
Of me.
Melting
Sunshine
Dreams of
Incense &
Candles Lit
To Replace
The Cold of
Past winters
Spent. I Love
You! Waxing
Bad distance
Of what Love
Was suppose
To be - to Set
My needy Heart
Free from its Memory!
Colder is this holder of reality that catches the pain of Mystery
To keep guessing the flicker of flame's insanity,
A harder coffin than life, a faster love to See
Than the wild spread forest Fire
Takes the unlit Tree!
Protected by Tears,
Rain, and the Sea,
Your Concrete Can Come
While My Ashes Can Leave,
This Volcano of ours leaves me no place to be,
But to Glow through the heat, never to flee, sparking eternal Destiny

# BE LEAVING

Having Faith In
Those Rulers
Which Colors
Through Thought
Hand Over
Made Love
Wet With
Conspiracies
That Manufacture Infrared Painted Walls Primed With An Undercoat Of
Translucent Compliance, Shallower Levels Of Discernible, Humanitarian
Connections, And A Fear Of Ostracized Embarrassment From Disclusive
Fangs Hungry
And Looming
Above These
Poor Peopled
Lands, Caped
By Dissipated
Governments
And Colluded
Ties Amongst
Continuously
Regenerating
Leaders With
Only Secular
Concerns For
Spiritual Will
Be A Wake &
Be Leaving In
DeathBeds!!!

# ANGEL'S ANGLES

A I
Fly By
You And
See By A
Little Bit of
Light SPEED Fixed
Sharp PIVOTING Points
Of View WINGS Over Un
To Micro — Waving
Glitching ALL Levelers
Caught Up In A Corner
Of The Eye Of God
Winking At Us
From Within
The Sub
Atomic
Dimension
Where There
Are No Units Of
Measuring Degrees
Where Reality Is Only
A Feather Pushing Down
The Wing of An Angel's
Perpetual Power In
Motility Defined
By A Language
Of Infinity

# 2 DUEL TO DO ALL DUALS

/\

1st—Take    In A 2nd    Take— 3
Some    You're    Good
Time    Out    Looks
To    To    Do
List    A    Rest
How    So    Well
I Am    Sad    By My
Self    Fee    Eye
Fish    You    Close
As    All    To
Many    Ways    Make
Do    Get    Up
Set Minds That Felt Like A Frayed Vagina Mite
Bug A Dickhead Poking Jokes In Her Net
-——-——MEMES——-——-
-——-—-MEANT-—-——-
-———ME!ME!———-
-——-SEE WE-——-
--—CAN BE—--
—THE NO—
-HOLDS-
-BARD-
SoLesS
WORN
In-OuT
WherE
WE'RE
FORKS
FORCE
SKINS
MEAN
WhilE
BEING
A BIT
OR LIP
OUTTA
WHAT?
It'S FoR
GettinG
OFF OR
SOME
THiNk
ELSE'S
WHAT
I GOT
YOU
\W/
?

# ToGetHer

Sweep Dreams
Up For Your Wisp Pouring
Lashing Liquor Lips Lended
Out The Love From Out Of
Beliefs Feelin' Less In Tune To
Carried Kinda A. I. Lazily Waving
Around Hatred Linking Notions
W/2Ton Can The Crappy
Feather Knot & Lost Catnaps
Weights Enter Twine Be Best
Getting Poet's Trees Nice &
Full ToGetHer For
Forever
& 4ever
2love
me
in
till
day
breaks
hour life
growing
non-stop
trophies
from the
surface of
the never
end—less
gerundive
phrases to
the tops of
sky stretch
mountains
2 nonsense
&tired vines
strike on the
grounds for fits
of the passion it
kisses us w/drizzle
&spits compliments
outwardly blooming
buds aloof
up on the roof
around&round we get
into a new home again
understanding growth!

# LEAF HOME

1st Try 2 Give A $2^{nd}$ Hand Me Downwards
2.Oh! Don't Point 2 A 4 Get The $5^{th\ The}$ Percent
The 40 & The 100 Proof Of Purchase Not Valid
In All 50 States Of The Read Write & Who
Matters          Spanning
Not To The $3^{rd}$ Eye Of A Beholder... See?
Side with the Many Multiple Organisms & An Organ
Is Um Or Gas Is Sum Found A Shunned Donation
Forced By The Times 2 Multiply Bear Foot And Pregnant
And Full Of Pregret Branch Out Of Your Comfy Zoned~Out
Head Out Of Your Mindlessnecessities! You Can't See
The Houses For The Homes With A Bird's Eye
Viewpointing Upon A
Growing Down
As A Race To
The Bottom
To Right Or
Be Wrong
All  Ways
We  Are
Used To
Growing
These In
Her Nestled Grasp At Wings Made Of     Dry Leaves A Dirty Idea Under Stood
Roots   ALL   Begot
The   SeedS   Aid
Planned   Bringing   In Evilish
Pair Renting   Life's   Small Feeling
Happiness   Free   From Airing
Out Of The   Dumb   Conceptually
Lil   Back   Wood   Made   In
Bit   Of   Being   Up   To
Split   It   From   In   Side
Us!

# The Roots Of The Poet Tree

Our Loose Leaf Paper Trailing Off The Beaten Pathological
Liars' Lips Waiting To Bark Better Like A Killer
Looking To Cover UP Half Of Life In The
Upper Case Study @ The Least End Side A
Dress Was Knotted Hairs To Your Part Of A
Singing Bunch A Bull Shit & It Won't Fly Anymore Than You're
Crappy Happy LoveBird Lying **Bee** Damned Foolish Dessert For Idiots
Like Me Too Used Up As The Hearts Attack One Or Another Over&Over&Out
Of Breathing Fumes Comes The New Tree Of Hope & Old Folk & Comfortable Eyes
Open In The Shades Of Understanding Places Timed Right From The Soul's For
Tunes Turned Up Barely Blaring The Most Passionately Voiced Ideas Of The
Satisfied Little Fart Can Be **Coming** More Sociable Turd Speeds
Returning To Its Nest To Sleep & Slips to The Ground
Up Safe Spotted W/Your Dead From Aging
Winter
To Grow
Down In—
Side Than
RIPPED
A-PART
AGAINST
MY Will &
Testament
Stumped!?
Not Yet
Branching
Confusion
Questions
No-No-No
Wings Itself
A Fishy Flopping About The Land W/One Wide Eye Up & One Winking Too Deeply!

# CuTuP

1 *A*
Po Po
Go Wit
Off All4
TaR Gets
Ring 2 Be 2
Races Points
Up To The Sun's
Setting Two
Times As
Decisive As
I Am Dangerous
Shining Sharper
Ways In Controlling
Me Are Bad Luck
Try Outs Fangs Cut
To Never Ending &
Happily Sever After

# NUMB BURS

OH... ONCE... I GOT YOU TO TALK TO ME AS
IF WE COULD TAKE IN OUR LOVELY
THOUGHT: THOSE OTHER CHANCES PAST AS
WAYS WE MAY BE
LOVE LIKE BE FOR
THAT FEELING AND RIGHT BEFORE ENDING

# THE DOWN—TIMES UP!!

Mister
Miss Us
Flipping
Birds Fly
A Fist Up
& Foisted
A Knuckled
Middleman
In All Mean
Directions
Point Out Half—Hour Of Our Power
Outages & Out Of The Tiniest Hands
Now He Handed Candy Hearts Round Usual
Time It's The Figuring Sweet&Salty Leaves Loving
The Best Indication Of Palms W/Sweat Soaked From A
Systemic Changing Nervous Necessary Leaching & Fostering
Fluidity In Nature Via Nurture Or Vice Versa Versus Versions
The World Can't Help But The Mad Unforeseeable Scratches
Courses Of Course A Coarse Future Caused By The Past Holes
Inaccurate Historic Fact-Checked Accounts Fall Into & Foreign
Institutions Of Higher Learning Lowering All Standards Of Living
Under The Universities' Universally & Selfishly Evil Elite Tests
Prescribed By The Administratively Inconspicuous Demons
Condescendingly Assuming That By Tainting Education
Under Their Oppressive Agenda To Impoverish As
Much Of The World's Population As They Can
Manipulate For Control Under The Guise
Of Arrogant Superiority Calls For The
Hands Of Many To Defend Children
Of The Good & Innocence! Off W/
Their Hands & Hard Heads! They
Think They're Smarter Than You!
Lil'Brother..? It's A. I. For An Eye!

# *THE SPACE-TIME CONTINUUM*

It's just about time! When the time is right, we're just in the nick of time. For old time's sake, from time to time & time after time & time & time again, it's that time of year again! And only to be certain that in time, time is on time, 100% of the time! Most times, time is most of the time & just in time before time runs out! It was a good time held by all—not like the last time! This time was the Last!

On the other hand (the hand of time) let the good times roll because times flies when you're having fun! You can't tell time; how many times must I tell you that? Only time will tell!!! And when it's time, a time will come! It won't be the first time! Those were some crazy times! There'll be plenty of time for a long time to come!

Wait! Time out! What time are we done? What time do we get off? Is it time to start? Is it *go* time? Or is it *time* to *go*? Is it quitting time! Or Overtime? Or double time? It's Miller time?

I think I need some time off!

It's High time to get a watch & watch the time go by in a timely fashion! You had a bad time because you have bad timing! For a time, you thought time was traveling through time! Well, time *is* kinda time traveling all the time! How many times do you suppose we'll have the whole time?

Time Times a zillion times? Until the end of time?

Where does all the time go?

In due time, time is money & I spent too much time wasting time. I can't buy us any more time! I try to make time on my own time but it just takes up so much of my free time. I can't find the time. I wish *Somebody* would just give me some time. I wish *someone* would at Least give me the time of day! It's a fine time to be asking for it, I know! I had the best time getting the best time on that timed test we took on times tables that time back in school in the time of my youth! Sometimes, in no time at all, time's awaiting?!?! And time waits for no man! Yet, you've got all the time in the world! I was trying to save us a little time! Ok? It's a fine time for that. Just take your time! I feel like for the time being, I just need some alone time... some time to myself... sometimes just to kill some time...! Because it's time you knew you were two timing me this whole time! So don't do the crime; if you can't do the time! If it happens another time, then it's time's up for my downtime! And next time'll be "Bedtime for Bonzo!"

But time is on my side & I had the time of my life! So thank you for your time & you're welcome! Anytime...!!! Because it was and is just a matter of time!!

# A CUTE DIRECT SHUN

Disentangling Your Synergy Is Not Happening Imaginatively
As If This Present Reality Happens 2
Be Unwrapped In Wards Wings Out
Side Spread Open Stretching The Sky
Lid Lifted With Eyes Surprised & Wild Absorbing A New Lover
Of The Unprotected Positions A Lush Mental Flower Pedal
Forward Taking Off Her Bow Over Laps
Goes Head 2 Head UpperHand Under
Where Secrets Were Unveiled To Each Quaint
Momentous Layer Down To These Detailed
Micro Motions Moving These
Hearts Turned Rhythmically
Off-Put Pushy Upbeat Steps
Synching Deeper Then Quickly The Rush Of The
Chorus First Arrives With Such Character Of A Choir
Fills The Gap W/Ugly Faces
Harmonious Making Love
Last Placed Into A Sound
Art Working To Please All Aesthetics Now Dripping Sweat Or Paint
On Improvised Voicings Of A Wet Outter-Worldly Godspelled Spoke
In Tongues Ambivalence
Like Screws Pronounced
Turning Tight Translations
By The Assertion Interrogated During A Consensually Bad Bed
Ex Changing Out Of Their Genes & Why Accede Knotty Lips
Now As Worn Out & Shaking
Memory Skirts Up FlashBacks
On Top Tits Out Sides Fracking
Themselves Amicably As Honest Sexually
Compensated Languid Beasts Sucking
Up Available Air Conditions Which
Plain CO2 Smoke Alarms The Lungs
Screens The Hope Less Than The Pain
Fool Soul's Testimony Teases Implications That Like 2 Demon
Eyes Using The Snickered Youth Of Yesterday's Allegations Lying
About Peaking At A Little More Over
All Costs Nothing But A Broad Under
Valued Higher W/ Standing Of Life As
A Nymph Foe Or Deal In The AfterMath Of A Parent Discounted Decisions

# SAiNTSAYiN'S

I
AM
THE
HERO
OF NOT
HINGING
ON THESE
HEROLDS OF
Having No —pastover— And Over
Underdogs Of A HOLIDAY'S A Traditionally
Created lore into a REALITY Despite ridicule's
Teased and forgotten CHECK Out of a level playing
Feel for what's what-not AND Field of what is supposed
To be or to become The BALANCE Between a good and evil
Forever and Everlasting Savior of a Love and Life to Live to Give
Upward and Out loudly freeing The company
Another's Last leg. A Sea's Limbering
Chance To Haunt Only Hell fire
To win A Holy Ghost Looks
At it W/out a float Too
USED FOR MARDI GRAS
PARADING AROUND NEW
ORLEANS OR PRICELESS
Beads to throw
To the kids We
Lift Laughing Are
Now raised and Held
Celebrated Like Immortal Stone
Figures IN History
THE
WAYS
KNOWN
to BE us
ALL
!

# AT LONG LAST

At Last Your Last Chance One Last Time The Last Dance
The Last One To Know The Last One In One Last Try
The Last Of The Mohicans The Last Man Standing
That's All Folks And That's The Last Of Them
The Last Call For Alcohol One Last Drink
The Last Second A Lasting Impression
Last Minute... Last Place... Last Night
Your Last Rights And Your Last Meal
The Last Day The Last Goodnight
Your Last Wish Goodbye
The Final Farewell
The Last Breath
The Last Stand
The Last Word
The Last Straw
The Last Poem
The Last Line
The Last Sip
The Last Of It
One Last Look
The Last Laugh
Every Last Drop
The Best For Last
That's The Last Of It
Every Last Little Bit Of It

# B A R S

She... Loves Me... Not As Much As We Had Once Felt
Her Having The Blind Attention 2 Hearts & Way Less
A-Way Out -ing Me By Spending More Time Safe W/O
Sourcing All The Scabs Over Our Claims 2 A Back—Up
Of The Best Ripped Off Thoughts SprucedUp Dates Pre
Poses With Scars And Taken At Face Value Paid 4 A
Kinky Stock By Sex You All... Miss Heard By A Last Take
King's Torn From Their Spells The Deadly Ear 4 Casting
Offers 2 Be Platonically Kin—Ship Mint To Be Wheather
What Was Deep Lips 2 Budge It Coming At Or 4 A 3
<u>Sum Times Counted Less Than 1 Admits 2 Of **The Bars** Were 8 4 2 & Then 1 By The Way Of Division</u>
Via Lovely Wording & There For Ambiguity Locks US In
Structures So At Odds W/Out A Conveying Side Most
Made This W/Out The Point To A Number OfAllThose
Reshaping Balance Of Anxiety's Setting Up HeldHands
A Mass A- PealingOut Takes On Sets A Bet Cuffed 2 A
Mounting Hung Or 4 Bartering W/A Sand Witch "1"
ReCounts 4 Skins Off The Hand Bag But 4 Gets How
Confusing My Back In Offering4 Bids The 4 Givin'Up A
Mortal Sin Forming A Fruit's Far More 2 Be Key Points
W/In This Sacrifice & In Tropic Dry Ice Pix Away Out

# THE BAR CODE

| | | | | |
|---|---|---|---|---|
| BEFORE WE | LOCK IT UP | BE FORGIVING | TO OUR NEW | -RESIDENTS- |
| VOLUNTEER | FOR NOW | AND THEN IN | CORRECTION | TO THOSE |
| LESS SOCIAL | WHEN WE | WORK CASES | OF THOUGHT | PROCESSED |
| EXPERIENCE | BROUGHT | AFTER CLASS | REASSIGNING | AS TALENT |
| WHY PEOPLE | ABOUT TO | TEST REFORM | MEDITATION | PROGRAMS |

THE NECESSITY FOR THAT WHICH BECOMES THE KEYSTROKES TO FIT EACH INDIVIDUAL'S CHARACTER SYMBLE NUMBER PUNCTUATION EMOTICON OR FORMAT IN THE CONTINUED TEXT WRITTEN BY THE PEOPLE'S UNITY!

| | | | | |
|---|---|---|---|---|
| IF YOU ARE | REFLECTING | MENTALLY AS | DESIGNED OR | PERSONALLY |
| USING THE | CONDITION | HYPNOBOTIC | PRESENTABLE | AS A TRANCE |
| ERRORDA-X | OF VIRTUAL | MANAGERIAL | PROCEDURAL | PROTOCOLIC |
| SIMULATED | ASSISTANCE | SCREENS ARE | ALLOWANCES | IN SYSTEMIC |
| COMPUTER | FORMATION | OBSERVED AS | IN BEHAVIOR | PROGRAMS* |

*SAID PROGRAMS ONLY FUNCTION IN ACCORDANCE TO THE NATIONAL-X INC. GOVERNMENTALLY APPROVED GUIDELINES AND/OR PROCESSES DIRECTLY ALIGNED W/NATIONAL-X INC. CIVIL CODE#O412BNAXSICUR2BN12

| | | | | |
|---|---|---|---|---|
| CIVILIANS | *MUST* PROVIDE* | ALL PROPER | PAPERWORK | FOR DOCTORS |
| GAIN THE | NEW MEDICALLY | REQUISITION | FROM FILES | IN ORDER OF |
| SHARING | ACCURATE INFO | IS FREEDOM | OF HEALTH & | LOCAL CARE'S |
| RECORDS | FOR ANY ILLNESS | & A UNIQUE | INDIVIDUAL'S | THERAPEUTICS |
| PATIENTS | PSYCHOLOGICAL | OR PHYSICAL | WELL—BEING | IS A PRIVILEGE! |

# —HYPN0-CRiTiCal—

——————The-Self————————————————Shilling-Refects————————————————The-Will——————
————Absorbed——————————————————One-An-0ther————————————————Within——0ut——————
———-Lasted-As——————————————————Long-As-Hell——————————————————Runs-Deep-——————
———Tattoos——————————————————AND/OR—————————————————Through Cuts-——————————
————0n-Fetal-Skin——————————————————Dying-Re——————————————Members-When——————————
——————Like-A-Rash————————————————Solution-4——————————————-Relationships-————————————
——————————Growing-————————————————- What-They——————————————Wanted-Was——————————
——————————H-E-A-V-Y————————————————Thought-As——————————-The-Trance——————————
——————————————-Formations——————————————2-HEAVY-2-Show————————————Furring-Ex——————————
———————————————-Spelled——————————————Color-0f-A——————————————Raise-0f——————————————
———————————————"A--D--D"——————————— Why? No————————————-Awareness-——————————————
————————————————————As-In-Math————Answers——————————0f-Insecurities-————————————————
—Many-Witch——————————————————Were-Apparent-When-A-Pair-Went-Walking A—Way-————————————————
——————A-Way————————————————-0ut-Wanting-To-Rent-0ut-An-Apartment With An-0ut-House————————
———————With-0ut-A-House—————————————— *IT'S ABOUT* ————————————————When-We-Were-0ut-——————
——————————(H-E-A-V-Y)———+++++++++++++++**** BLANK ****+++++++++++++++——————————————(H-3-A-V-Y)——————
————————————A-Pear-Rant!-A-Parent Wondered —ʊ— Why-Women-Appear-Pear-Shaped-——————————Walking-Away—
————————————————————Who-Was-Gone-Too-(HEAVY)-Peeping-A-Hole-In-The-Sub——————————————————
——————————————————Conscious——————————Atomic——————————————-Terrane——————————————————
——————————————————0f-A-Pet ——————————-Tee ——————————————————Doggie——————————————————
——————————————————-Project——————————————Top——————————————————Style-Let-——————————————————
——————————————2-Mine 0r——————————————Notched——————————————————Up-End-——————————————————
——————————————————Deal——————————————————Inn——————————————————DusT-Tree-——————————————————
——————————————————-Lures——————————————————Arms——————————————————HEAVY——————————————————
——————————————————-0ver——————————————————Bear——————————————————-Ring-——————————————————
——————————————-Acts-A——————————————————Foot——————————————————In-Sur-——————————————————
————————————-Round——————————————————-Sounds——————————————————Real-——————————————————
——————————About——————————————————Cold——————————————————Hard-——————————————————
————————Truth——————————————————Towing——————————————————Facts——————————————————

# LOOK-OUT-LOOKS-INTUIT

WATCH A CROSS SIGNALS
OBJECTS — - .-. - — BEAMED
— . . . — — — . . . —
A LIGHT — — — MINUTE
- — - - — -
NEAR BY - POLOR ELECTRIC CURRENTS CONTRACT AND BUCK - SHOCKS OF
- —BULLHORNS JOISTING @ OUR VICINITY FROM A— -
FURTHER - REDDENING TERROR OF THOSE ULTRAVIOLET EYES - BLINKING
- . — ONCE CALLED OUR INEVITABLE TALE A COLLECTIVE — . -
UNHAPPY END TO THIS MORTALLY FAKE REALITY'S SYNAPSES CHANGE IN
- - — WE PERCEIVED FROM THIS MICROSCOPIC CORNER — - -
DIMENSIONS OF THE KNOWN UNIVERSE AND NOW WE CAN SEE PASSING THE
- - — —LOOKS OF DESPERATE HATRED IN THE BULL'S EYES— — - -
CRY-WOLVES AROUND THE DIMMING CENTERS OF GALAXY-LIKE VIEWS FROM
- - — —EVER-MADDENING MEGA-MINOTAUR'S EYES AND— — - -
DEADLIEST IS THE ENCROACHING SPEED OF INFRARED LIGHTS INSIDE THIS
- - — MASSES OF FLAME FLOATING UPON DARK WATER — - -
RUSHING IN -ROTATING W/A BLACK EDGE & SUCKING INTO SUB- STANCE OF
- NUCLEOTIDAL WORLD-PULLING WHIRLPOOL THEN -
SELFISHLY - _—GENETICALLY-GRIFTING POLYMERIC GADFLIES DID—_ - DEMONIC
_— FLUSH INTO SOME NEW TRANSMUTATED ARENA? —_
WEIGHS—OUT — — — — — WAYS—OUTTA
— — — — —
GRAVITY — - — — — - — FORCES
- - - — — - - -
*LIVES* TO WAIT UNTIL AN INFINITY OF ALL-TIMES TO RUN
- - — - -
OUT ON GOD'S ETERNAL EXISTENCE!!!

# FUNNYBONE

Those Hip-Bone's Connections Ties
Mans-Laughter I Sent You All! *Youth* & Truth
Gnawing Into Ligamental Pork Poking Ribs' Is Chewing At Me Fun-Duh?-Mentally! Yes! I Affirmed It!
Facto...! Via.. Able? & Viable!! Check & Make Sure Before You Checked Out You Check Out All Of The
Checkpoints Gone Unchecked; Checking Amounts To Nothing But W/A Bad Check & W/A Check-Oh-
SLO-Vod-Kia? Drinking Problem In Check! & Mate? But Hmmm! I Adderol... But I Methed-It-All-Up!!!
It's A Damned Thing... I'd Started To Long For
Attention I Forgot That I Didn't Want

# I SPYDAR

LET'S TUCK HER INTO A COMFORTABLE CELL. COMATOSE HELL. ROAST. YOU'RE BOTH WELCOME!
OH WAKE UP **W/OUT** NO ARMS TO
GET HER IN **THE BED** NO MORE DAYS
HER ONLY **ACT**-IS AS IF-**SHE**/ FOOLS HER
SELF WHEN **SHE** **FELT** WITH A HAND
FULL IT'S AT **ONCE** **STIFF** SEXUAL DESIRES
FILLED & 1ST—**MADE**—INTO POINTS OF—**VIEWS**—EYE AN OTHER
USED UP & **ABOUT** **WHICH** ONE'S SKIN
IS LOSING **HOW IT** **WRAPS** DEEPER IN
OUT—**LASTED** **INSIDE**—HER
**WASN'T**—THE SOUL OF A MESS EMPTY NEST—**UNREAL**
**KNOWN** **DREAMS**

# Upper
# Down

As So
Above Benign
Hyper Act To Be Low
Or Like Stank Key Bored Of
Asphalt Doesn't Target Roadkills
Smell Battered For Rested On The Run
A Weighed Down Deep Gloom Laden W/Sudden Unanticipated Joyful Blasts Of Viciously Hilarious GoodTimes
<-& Bad Timing. I Ache For Tepid Peace While Innovative Technology Becomes Narcissistic Paraphernalia In Ever->
Shallowing Kiddie Pools Of Cultural Muck. I Draw A Blank In Visible Ink. My Scrappy Heart Rattles Naked From
My Skull, Dragging Behind Th'Waggon
Dyslexia Raging @Attn: Left The
Flying Under Ground Fore
The Radar Cited Shot
Gun Is Hurtin'
All Us

# U-TURN STYLE

So Please
Do Not Give Me
A Lot Of Sneaky Ways To Get To
Piece Your Go-To kNow Where
To/Fit\In Two Days From When
W/AWitch's Ways From A Diss Cussed
Brewing The Upper Most Portion Out Your HATE\-
Full Attack Modes Often Ate Up & LEFT YOU/'
W/Out Twisted Rational Reasoning
Ideas Together Turns Tiles Over
Puts Up W/In S C A L E S
Us Down In Your
LOVINGRIP

# DAYMOON

All These Fringe Circles Moved Entropy Around
Wills Turn Back Door's
Locks Into A Broken Open
Safe Light From Eyes
Only Fire Works With
This That That Love
Bent Over Time Less
Looks Stretched Ends
Past Rain Falls And
Never Drops Outta Sight
Minds Who Play Ain't
Gotta Beat With Pure
Heart Black Gold Lasting
Longer As You Dust Words
Lost To Be Analog Grips On The Edge Of Eternity

# KisS2kisS

He held Her head<br>
Back. He Was Love.<br>
Had . . . He made<br>
Sense**?** **A** gesture<br>
Perhaps, Of questions<br>
To her eyes He was held in, for<br>
She saw the answers No good reasons . . .<br>
But their Lips moved into smiles**&**touched as their Eyelids closed<br>
A—way to sleep in feeling So they had envisioned<br>
This biting at her at his frightened chance to happy himself-then-<br>
Came so close to becoming ***1*** Letting go of fear and of<br>
Each other's Scars and<br>
Hearts= Love!

# Epilogue

Similar to bonus footage for a film, shown after the credits roll, I've decided to add another passage and another poem. Except I haven't written the poem yet, and after I have written it, I'm going to attempt (to the best of my abilities) to interpret the poem, its poetic devices, and whatever conscious, subconscious, preconscious, or unconscious thematic and emotional meaning that I can extrapolate from it. I only presently have its title and a vague, mental image of its shape in mind. The poem will be titled "Ghost Note," and the idea behind it is that it will be a metaphor for itself and its function as a, hopefully, good-enough piece of art to speak for me and express my love for it and creating it, my love of poetry as well as art in general, and also I'll attempt to express some love for myself (dangerously traversing a fine-lined, balancing act of self-awareness while not portraying myself as too pompous, hyperbolic, hypocritical, condescending, arrogant, too cynical, too contrived, too self-critical, silly, or overly egotistical while trying to remain humble, honest, freshly original, yet true to my voice and style as a poet and artist)! Ha…! Of course, I'm aware of the vain pursuit of it all! I presently know that I might be the only person in the world who'll ever see this passage and/or poem if I don't like it!

Finally, as I approach this seemingly unique, very uncomfortable, possibly embarrassing, and extremely odd exercise in writing, I want to thank you, the reader! I'd be lying if I said there wasn't a substantial part of me that isn't writing this section for myself and my love for the process, but in all seriousness and sincerity, if you are reading this, THANK YOU! This *is* for *YOU!!!* More so than it is for me! It means EVERYTHING to me to have an audience of any caliber! Even if it's just you! And I can only pray to God that something I write moves you, personally, and perhaps helps connect you to the whole human experience and it's complications and all of its wonderful possibilities and beauty! Remember! There are no real rules in art! Only what satisfies you, whether you create or consume it! Both aspects take a certain level of sophistication and active participation! Both sides of this reflective coin are equal in my heart and understanding of art! I do this for me and you, and I'm compelled to entertain, create, and hopefully make you think in a way that uplifts your understanding of existence and life, itself, as I try my best to dissect it and discern the mundane from the most important hidden aspects of that which may seem so unimportant in its attributable nature as well as the most exciting aspects of any vibrant, immediate artistic piece of the medium of life! So, again, THANK YOU SO VERY MUCH!!! I appreciate you taking this journey with me!

Although, I am currently alive, this poem, "Ghost Note," will act as my gift to, connection with, and communication between the reader and myself with the poem playing as a metaphysical Rosetta Stone.

The title, "Ghost Note," has a couple of meanings. The obvious one: It's a note from my ghost to the reader; a hopeful sign that my poetry will outlive me. I have no evidence of this. This book will be my first publication. It will be self-published, and as far as I can tell, it will be self-promoted! I'm going to have to address this issue in the poem, itself, but I don't intend on presenting a "message in bottle" type of theme to result from this poem; I am going to write confidently as I always intend to do when I write! I know I said "this and that" about all the egotistical trappings that I'm going to attempt to avoid involving this endeavor, but that doesn't mean I don't write with confidence and passion! I don't know how one can do one without the other? And I'll be writing till it's my time to "shuffle off this mortal coil!"

"Ghost Note" is also a music term and I'll be incorporating this idea thematically as well as through imagery as best I can! I also was drawn to this idea heavily by this analogy between music and the rhythm of poetry! I rarely write in poetic meter but there is a definite rhythm in my poetry! Being a fairly decent guitarist and musician as an amateur composer, I'm going to search for a strong heartbeat in this piece! Not necessarily a rhyme scheme or a fixed meter but a fluent and noteworthy musical feeling. I'd like to add that this musical premise is what I'm most excited about exploring here! So we'll see what happens with this aspect of the poem! In fact, I think I'm gonna dive write into the poem right away! This is becoming more and more invigorating as I discover my intentions! It feels very raw and kinda Jack Kerouac-like just freestyling this passage! Yet, we'll see how "stream of consciousness-like" I leave the final product. I'm a picky little self-editor! I can toy with the micro-positioning of characters and punctuation, alone, for hours on end, so… wish me luck! Wink wink!! (20 minutes later…!)

Wow! Ok that was fast, and not at all what I was expecting from the poem or myself! It was fluid. Wet. Painted like Jackson Pollock but with e.e. Cummins dropping on the canvas! I think I'm going to play with the shape of the poem some more, but I'm very pleased with my amoeba-like syntax and the "off-the-top" and "fast-dropped" lexicon. As for the structure of the poem, I'm going to leave the words in their original order by line and in series, but I'm thinking that I see a picture between the lines, coming from the blank spots of white spaces between the words! I believe this is where my ghost is hiding! (Days later: I decided to change the word 'use' from 'you' to rationalize the use of "Re—" in the preceding line to cement its dualistic qualities and the two possible paths the reader can take separately.

Otherwise, the poem has not changed nor will.)

"Ghost Note" is very surrealistic by execution, so I don't know how much I can interpret it for you. I know that sounds lackluster, but it's not often that I reach such a level of meta-conscious abstraction! This was especially true and beneficial considering the amount of pre-interpretation that I laid out for you.

After rereading the poem later, I believe that I at least owe you an explanation of some of my artistic decisions because the message and meaning seems abundantly clear to me and what, at first glance, seemed like normal aesthetics to my eyes became more evident in afterthoughts. Firstly, I rearranged the position of multiple words and nothing came from that venture. Then, in that second look, I realized the reason the shape of the poem should remain abstract, albeit semi-painfully, is due to the lack of incompatibility between the two sides of the poem, which are so close in proximity and in their structural makeup of straight lines and sharp angles that they seem destined to fit. On the contrary, straight lines aren't natural, they're constructed by man. This poem is purposefully forced. The ghost note is unnatural. The ghost is comfortable in but doesn't fit into the realm of the reader. The diagonal lines are straight but all of their angles are slightly off from each other. In some places through the center it looks as though one side will puzzle piece into the other, but this is not consistent. This look of initial similarity broken by a second inspection of the two halves of the poem continues as the outsides of the poem also defy consistency. Some uniformity here and there only pushes a notion that the poem has a structural purpose without the payoff of actually having one. The reasoning behind this idea follows a disconnect between the reader and writer, life and the spiritual, the divine and the ordinary, and also between art and the artist himself! All of these ideas are presented by my inability to grasp what I set out to do. Instead of showing the connections between these types of subjects and embracing them. I can only marvel at Pollock's work without fully knowing if I get it! (Or if there is anything to get!) This allows that healthy skepticism to creep back into all art, be it mine or historic. Also, if you're following what I mean by this visual interpretation and you follow the path down through the center of the poem, there is a quick exit to the left of the poem between lines three and four. It's the path for those who only admire the superficialities of art and would rather ignore the deeper substance of artwork or their slippery ideas that aren't easily accessible to those who don't normally subscribe to them.

Syntactically, the text follows some of the same patterns of disjunction. The "A." in the second to last line was a happy accident produced by the auto correct function of my device; I immediately liked it and changed the word, "Be," to "B." adding the second instance of a bullet point list denoted by the two letters. Ironically, in reading the poem completely across and down, the "B" comes before the "A" which further indicates a disconnect between the two sides of the poem. (It's alphabetically correct reading order still visually pits the two bullet points at equal but opposite sides of the two halves of the text!)

I think the "blue eye" should stand out being the only lowercased line of verse. This is the small, overlooked eye of the artist. Sad in youth and beauty or lack thereof from time and loss of life. In the ghost's subconscious, his awareness is fleeting, not perceiving half of the things he's describing. The only sounding of an actual ghost note in the poem is the "plop" of colors and paint that the narrator can't feel. Here, it's not clear if he's imagining an implied sound. Perhaps the song is just stuck in his head? The repetition of the word, "no," and its final misused substitute for the word, "know,"' is the ghost's subconscious reinforcement of this disconnection between realities, aesthetic understanding, and the heart of the audience. This creeping realization briefly surfaces as he questions, "no?" before beginning the checklist of examples to combat this realization. The mirror gives off the wrong impression, like these two worlds reflect one another but not in the way in which the observer or artist can recognize. The vampire is ghostly but can still see his own body and without reflection, either introspectively or superficially, he still exists to communicate the essence of life. The "stares up" is a play on words but also refers to the living being's subconscious awareness of the ghost's presence, completing this paralleled dance between these disconnects, affirming that same ole lifelong, ever-existing search for meaning in life and wrestling with a lack of proof for something else beyond this existence.

Emotionally, the poem feels very good in spirit. A sense of ease and security seemed to wrap around me while writing it! I directly mention Pollock in the text so that painting/poetry analogy is quite evident. I also held a vague image of Michelangelo's "The Creation of Adam" in my head through the initial creation of "Ghost Note." That image along with a few mental composites of Pollack's "Automatic Art" style of drip painting while visualizing a few fluid-like puzzle pieces morphing so closely around each other, like oil in water, represents the small yet infinitely vast space between the artist and the observer, the unknown and the imagined, and that of Man and God's fingers in "The Creation of Man!" I was a ghost in the room of the poem. I hope the reader will know I'm there with them and in them whenever they spend some time with the poem! Thank You again! Enjoy!!!!!

—Jason Brenton Gore
Wednesday, October 31, 2023

# GHOST NOTE

This is BOLD All CAPSold
I've got Jackson Pollock Dripping on me B. His Bloody
blue eye Drops Yellow & Red paint
Goes through me I am translucent
The colors are real The plop on cement
With a sound I can't feel! Everyone there can't see me
On the other hand Stretching fingers pointing
I cannot see me either Not like a vampire biting the shine
Side of the Mirror Projection of one Side
I see Clearer
No Lite
No Fear
To Re-
Use Flex
NoT On
Much more than An Eye Floater
A Fly is going over I'm elated at the site you all
Ways to recall Ready talk 0r go
With Out
A Mouth
Zero… Cold case
On the floor I am born in
Mine…. Re— Mind
Oh whoa slow down ok let go… You know my soul is on this place like
Yesterday's on this page, ya no? The stares up show
A. Autumn Attics
Ghost Note

# ABOUT THE AUTHOR

Jason Brenton Gore was born in Natchez, Mississippi on January 18, 1975. He spent his childhood, there and 5 minutes away, across the Mississippi River in Vidalia, Louisiana. At age 11, he moved with his mother to Plano, Texas and spent the remainder of his adolescence living with relatives between his place of origin in the "Miss-Lou" and the Dallas area. He attended Louisiana State University, where he received a Bachelor's in English Creative Writing. Jason currently lives in New Orleans, Louisiana as a writer and musician.

Made in the USA
Columbia, SC
13 February 2024